Employment and Labour Market Interventions

Employment and Labour Market Interventions

Papers and Proceedings of the
Fourth Meeting of Asian Employment Planners,
New Delhi, December 17-19, 1991

ILO-ARTEP

Asian Regional Team For
Employment Promotion (ARTEP)

World Employment
Programme

First Printed 1992

ISBN: 92-2-108551-1

Preface

The rapid structural changes in most Asian countries and the emphasis on export-oriented industrialisation strategy have greatly influenced production systems, carrying implications for employment, wages, labour standards and industrial relations. On the one hand firm level restructuring has led to changing occupational structure of employment, changing skill needs and flexibility in forms of employment. Increasing deregulation of labour markets on the other hand has tended to relegate the role of long-term manpower planning and skills development. Labour market analysis has acquired added significance in recent years.

These issues and the experiences of Asian economies were presented for discussion at the Fourth Meeting of Asian Employment Planners organised by the ARTEP in New Delhi on 17-19 December, 1991. The fourth in a series of biennial meetings held by the ARTEP, this Meeting provided a forum for senior officials of the ministries of labour and planning as well as representatives of employers and workers organisations of the Asian region and also international agencies to discuss key employment issues facing the countries of the region. In addition ARTEP's Programme of Work for the next two years was examined with the intention of focussing on priority areas for technical assistance and advisory services.

Senior planners from 14 Asian countries including Bangladesh, Bhutan, Brunei, the People's Republic of China, India, Indonesia, Lao PDR, Malaysia, Mongolia, Nepal, Pakistan, Philippines, Sri Lanka and Thailand participated in the Meeting. In addition there were representatives from workers and employers organisations, senior officials from ILO headquarters in Geneva, and the ILO Regional Office in Bangkok and a resource person from the U.K. (for the List of Participants see Annex).

The present volume puts together the papers presented and the discussions that followed at the Meeting. A brief exposition of the major items of ARTEP's Programme of Work for 1992-93 as presented by Dr. Rizwanul Islam, Director, ARTEP and ratified by the participants is also contained in the volume.

The volume contains the four theme papers namely, (i) *Labour Shortage as an Aim of Employment Strategy: An Overview of Trends and Prospects in Developing Asia* by Martin Godfrey; (ii) *Labour Market Analysis and Human Resources Development* by M. Muqtada; (iii) *Education, Training and Employment: What Can Planners Do?* by Martin Godfrey; and (iv) *Interventions in Rural Labour Markets: Some Asian Experiences* by Piyasiri Wickramasekara. All four papers have an underlying emphasis on aspects of employment, income, and poverty alleviation.

New Delhi,
July 1992   ILO-ARTEP

Contents

1

Labour Shortage as an Aim of Employment Strategy: An Overview of Trends and Prospects in Developing Asia[1]

MARTIN GODFREY

Although shortage of labour is often discussed as if it were a problem, it is a problem that the governments of most developing countries must devoutly wish they were facing. Indeed, the achievement of a *real* labour shortage, with rising real wages reflecting increases in productivity, should be seen as the proper, ultimate aim of employment strategy, a cause for celebration rather than worry. In this respect several of Asia's most dynamic developing economies already have plenty to celebrate, and several others are showing signs of being on the road towards the same destination. This paper attempts to track the progress along this road of the region's various economies and to explore prospects of further progress. This attempt is hindered by unsatisfactory measurement concepts and procedures, and an alternative approach is suggested for this purpose.

1.1 Recent Trends in Asian Developing Economies

The two years since the last meeting of Asian Employment Planners, in November 1989, have been relatively good ones for most of Asia's developing economies, in spite of recession in most industrialised economies, as Table 1 shows. While slower than in 1988, economic growth in developing Asia was much faster than in the rest of the world.[2]

In the newly industrialising economies (NIEs) growth slowed down in this period but they still achieved an annual average growth rate in real GDP per head of over 5 per cent in 1989 and 1990.

In Hong Kong the main dampening factor was uncertainty about prospects after 1997, but slower growth in export markets, weak domestic demand and a very tight labour market (encouraging relocation of low-wage manufacturing to China) also had an effect, only partly offset by growth in services and construction;

---

1. In the writing of this paper, extensive assistance was provided by Mritiunjoy Mohanty.
2. This section and sections 1.2 and 1.5.2 draw heavily on Asian Development Bank (1991).

TABLE 1

Indicators of Recent Trends in Selected Asian Economies

	GNP per head ($) 1989	Population (mn) 1989	Ann. avg. growth rate real GDP pc 1989 and 90 %	Ann. avg. growth rate agriculture 1989 and 90 %	Ann. avg. growth rate industry 1989 and 90 %	Ann. avg. growth rate services 1989 and 90 %	Ann. avg. growth rate export earnings 1989 and 90 %
Newly Industrialising Economies							
Hong Kong	10320	70.9	5.3	—	—	—	9.0
Korea, Rep.	4400	5.8	1.0				14.6
Singapore	10450	42.4	6.4	0.0	7.6	8.8	3.6
Taiwan–China	7510	2.7	6.8	-5.1	7.8	9.5	13.9
		20.0	5.2	-0.3	2.9	10.2	4.9
South East Asia		380.8	5.8	—	—	—	17.1
Indonesia	490	179.1	5.0	3.4	8.2	8.2	14.9
Lao PDR	180	4.1	7.0	5.3	25.5	11.2	10.5
Malaysia	2130	17.4	5.8	4.8	11.9	8.5	17.4
Philippines	700	60.4	1.8	3.3	4.4	4.4	7.7
Thailand	1160	55.5	9.3	1.9	16.6	10.3	21.8
Vietnam, Soc. Rep.	200	64.4	2.9	3.8	1.4	9.1	42.2
South Asia		1104.9	2.6	—	—	—	13.3
Bangladesh	180	109.1	2.0	3.3	5.9	4.8	8.4
India	350	811.8	2.6	2.4	6.4	5.8	15.1
Myanmar	200	40.0	4.3	8.2	11.3	2.4	49.6
Nepal	170	18.4	-0.4	4.8	—	—	-4.3
Pakistan	360	108.7	2.0	4.8	5.5	4.3	7.0
Sri Lanka	430	16.8	2.3	0.8	6.5	3.6	11.5
China, People's Rep.	360	1106.4	3.0	5.0	8.1	—	11.7

(contd.)

TABLE 1 (contd.)

Indicators of Recent Trends in Selected Asian Economies

	GNP per head ($) 1989	Population (mn) 1989	Ann. avg. growth rate real GDP pc 1989 and 90 %	Ann. avg growth rate agriculture 1989 and 90 %	Ann. avg. growth rate industry 1989 and 90 %	Ann. avg. growth rate services 1989 and 90 %	Ann. avg. growth rate export earnings 1989 and 90 %
Pacific Islands	—	5.1	-0.6	—	—	—	-7.6
Fiji	1640	0.7	8.1	7.5	10.2	9.1	13.8
Papua New Guinea	900	3.6	-3.8	0.5	-4.2	-0.9	-13.5
Solomon Islands	570	0.3	3.1*	8.8	5.0	3.0	-7.2
Tonga	910	0.1	1.1*	1.3	2.1	1.2	16.6
Vanuatu	860	0.2	1.0*	9.5	6.3	2.8	-6.3
Western Samoa	730	0.2	0.7*	—	—	—	-18.5
These Asian Countries	—	2668.0	4.1	—	—	—	11.0
All Developing Countries	—	4123.0	2.6	—	—	—	—
All Developed Countries	—	750.1	3.0	—	—	—	—

Notes: —not available
          * 1989 only

Source: Asian Development Bank (1991), Tables A2, A3, A4, A5, A13 and A30.

the 1 per cent real growth rate per head in 1989 and 1990, shown in Table 1, compares with a rate of nearly 7 per cent in 1988.

In the Republic of Korea the deceleration was less spectacular, from 10 to 6 per cent, with agriculture stagnant and industry and services growing but at a slower rate than in recent years. Appreciation of the currency and rapid increases in wages caused problems in foreign markets, and export growth averaged only 4 per cent over 1989 and 1990, the first time in three decades that this growth rate has fallen below 10 per cent.

Singapore did the best of the NIEs in this period, with very fast growth of business and financial services compensating for slower growth of industry (dependent on exports, particularly to the US). The transition to a high-value-added, services-based economy was further encouraged by tax rebates to multinational corporations basing their financial services in Singapore and to foreign exchange traders, an increase in the ceiling on foreign equity participation in local banks, and the lifting of the ban on the provision of domestic banking services by foreign banks.

As in the case of Korea, Taiwan-China's export earnings were hit by currency appreciation and rising labour costs. As a result industrial growth almost stopped in 1990, and only fast expansion of the services sector kept the economy on the move. The stock and property markets collapsed in 1990, and a large outflow of capital (amounting to over 6 per cent of GDP) reflected a weakening of investment opportunities at home.

With growth slackening in the NIEs, South East Asia took over as the region's most dynamic grouping, with average growth rates over the past two years only marginally below that achieved in 1988.

The Malaysian economy, one of the most dynamic in the world, actually grew slightly faster in 1989-90 than in 1988, with industry (both domestic and export-oriented) and services especially buoyant. High levels of domestic and foreign investment (the latter particularly from Taiwan-China, China and Japan) have fuelled the Malaysian boom, and recent increases in oil revenues have been useful.

The region's fastest growing economy over this period, however, remained Thailand, even though rising oil prices and slackening external demand cut the growth rate from its 1988 peak. Exports and industrial output, in particular, grew at phenomenal rates, as did the construction sector. Monetary policy was tightened in the second half of 1990 to check inflationary pressures, but the investment boom continued, with foreign investors attracted by low-cost labour and expanding domestic as well as export markets.

Indonesia finally reaped the benefit of its tough structural adjustment measures, with an annual average growth in export earnings of 15 per cent reflecting an even higher rate of growth in manufactured exports. The services sector also expanded fast, partly in response to the deregulation of the financial system. A welcome result of the recent export success is a decline in the external debt service ratio (which had risen to a worrying 35 per cent) to 28 per cent.

The Philippines remains an economy of great potential but so far limited achievement. Natural and political calamities aggravated persistent macro-economic imbalances over this two-year period, to produce one of the region's lowest growth rates. Drought followed by typhoons hit agricultural production, while disruption of power supplies, increases in wages and interest rates and recession in export markets slowed manufacturing growth. Since mid-1990 the economy has had to cope with an earthquake, the Gulf crisis and a major volcanic eruption. An attempted coup at the end of 1989 further weakened business confidence. At the same time, little progress has been made with implementation of economic reforms, and external indebtedness is still high.

Two South East Asian economies in the process of even more fundamental adjustment, from central planning to markets, are Vietnam and Lao PDR. Vietnam experienced slower growth in 1989-90 than in 1988 but still enjoyed an export boom (mainly in rice and crude oil). The disruption of credit and inputs from the CMEA countries has caused problems, and the rate of price inflation, which had appeared to be under control in 1989, has moved up again, partly because state enterprises still have access to subsidised loans from the government. Lao PDR has become one of the region's most dynamic economies, with fast agricultural growth reflecting improved weather conditions and incentives, and feeding even faster growth in (largely agro-based) industry, which also benefited from economic reforms. The flaw in the growth process is the low rate of domestic saving, which has led to dependence on concessional foreign aid and inflationary deficit financing.

China is in the throes of a similar but more protracted reform process. Growth was deliberately slowed in 1989 and 1990, through drastic cuts in investment, but rates were still quite high. A strong recovery in the second half of 1990 was led by the non-state sector, particularly rural collectives amd foreign-funded enterprises, to the benefit of exports. The economy remains one of the fastest growing in the world (well on its way to quadrupling its 1980 output by the year 2000), but it is plagued by recurrent macro-economic instability.

South Asia is often regarded as the continent's most problematic sub-region, and its growth has slowed in the past two years, but the annual average growth rate in income per head of almost 3 per cent is still a respectable achievement in current circumstances.

In India the extraordinarily high growth rate achieved in 1988 proved impossible to maintain. A recovery that was getting under way in 1990 was interrupted by the Gulf crisis. As usual industry was the fastest growing sector, with services not far behind. Exports (of which almost three-quarters are now manufactured goods) continued to do well, helped by the steady real devaluation of the rupee, but imports also grew fast, and both trade and current account deficits increased in 1990. The resulting depletion of foreign exchange reserves and increase in external borrowing, together with the persistently high budget deficit, necessitated resort to IMF assistance and structural adjustment reforms.

The IMF and structural adjustment reforms are also in evidence in Pakistan, where growth has slowed in the past two years. The large-scale industrial sector has been particularly sluggish, as a result not only of its own inefficiency but also of infrastructure bottlenecks, political uncertainty and breakdowns in law and order. Agriculture had a bumper year in 1989 but input supply problems held back growth in 1990. Export expansion was at a lower rate than in recent years, largely due to a decline in exports of primary commodities. Manufactured exports still did well, but continued dependence on a few items (synthetic textiles, cotton yarn and cloth, and garments) is worrying.

In 1990 Bangladesh showed what it might achieve if spared the constant buffeting of natural disasters, and recorded the highest economic growth rate in South Asia. Agriculture led the way, thanks to improved policies as well as favourable weather, and the target of food self-sufficiency was in sight. The resulting increase in internal demand boosted industrial output, while exports of garments, jute and jute goods, leather and shrimps also increased. However, with its low rate of domestic saving, the economy remains overwhelmingly dependent on foreign resources, and vulnerable to shocks, both natural and man-made.

Accelerating growth in Sri Lanka has led to (perhaps premature) talk of an economic miracle. Improvements in the weather, the security situation and government policies were reflected in a surge of activity in 1990, in agriculture, industry and tourism. In industry the private sector did particularly well, with substantial increases in output of textiles, chemicals and metal products. Substantial increases in exports of tea, garments, processed gems and petroleum products, and in receipts from tourism, brought an improvement in the current account balance in spite of the Gulf crisis. Foreign investors have renewed their interest in the Sri Lankan economy but are watching the security situation carefully before making large commitments.

The picture of economic stagnation in the Pacific Islands over the past two years largely reflects the problems of Papua New Guinea, where GDP actually fell as a result of the continued closure of the Bougainville gold and copper mine, weaker world commodity prices and lower export volumes. Fiji, on the other hand, had two years of remarkable growth, to which agriculture, industry (particularly manufactured exports) and tourism all contributed.

All in all, then, these were good years for most developing economies in the Asian region, which continued to be the fastest growing region in the world, in spite of the impact of the Gulf crisis, discussed in more detail in the next section.

1.2   The Impact of the Gulf Crisis

The crisis in the Gulf in 1990–91 sent shock waves through several Asian economies and labour markets, particularly those of Bangladesh, Sri Lanka, Pakistan, India and the Philippines. In a series of rapidly mounted studies[1] ILO–ARTEP was able to assess the immediate impact of the crisis in some of the worst affected areas.

The annual rate of gross migration from Bangladesh to the Middle East had reached over 97,000 by 1990, and there were estimated to be 90,000 Bangladeshi workers in Kuwait and Iraq by August of that year. By February 1991 some 65,000 of these were estimated to have returned home (equivalent to about 0.2 per cent of the total Bangladeshi labour force). A large proportion of those returning is likely to have some skills; 39 per cent of those moving to Kuwait and 85 per cent of those moving to Iraq in 1989–90 had been estimated to be professional, semi-professional or skilled workers. But that still left a sizeable number of semi-skilled and unskilled workers to be reabsorbed into local labour markets. At the same time, remittances, which had been running at over $100 million a year from the two countries through official channels alone, fell to zero.

---

1.   ILO-ARTEP (1990a, 1990b, 1991a, 1991b).

Sri Lanka had an even larger number of migrant workers in Iraq and Kuwait, over 100,000 out of a total in the Middle East of nearly 300,000. As an immediate result of the crisis, 96,000 were identified as stranded (equivalent to 1.6 per cent of the total Sri Lankan labour force), to be repatriated to Sri Lanka or found alternative employment in adjacent countries, particularly Saudi Arabia. Almost two-thirds of the country's workers in the Gulf were unskilled, so reabsorption posed a difficult problem, aggravated by reduced levels of out-migration as a result of the crisis. Also, remittances are estimated to have been $44 million lower than otherwise in 1990.

Of about 95,000 Pakistani workers in Kuwait and Iraq at the onset of the crisis, almost 70,000 (equivalent to only about 0.2 per cent of the total Pakistani labour force) had been repatriated by the end of 1990. Most of these (79 per cent) were in the occupational category, production and related workers, transport operators and labourers, but were relatively highly educated (43 per cent with Matric and above). They posed a special problem of resettlement partly because of their ability to form associations and lodge their demands in an organised manner (ILO-ARTEP, 1991:35). They were also geographically concentrated, with 52 per cent from Punjab province. Kuwait and Iran accounted for 9 per cent of remittances from Pakistanis abroad, and those from Kuwait alone amounted to $170 million in 1988-89.

Of the South Asian countries, India had the largest number of workers in Iraq and Kuwait, and the total number of its displaced migrants was estimated at 137,000. This is not large in relation to the Indian labour force (only about 0.05 per cent), or the number on the register of employment exchanges (0.5 per cent), but regional concentration was heavy. The number of migrant workers returning to Kerala alone may have been as high as 80,000, equivalent to more than 10 per cent of total public and private employment in the state. The proportion of skilled-and-above workers among returnees was estimated to be as high as 60 per cent, and only about 10 per cent of them were estimated to be in serious financial trouble. Nevertheless, the problem of reabsorption was a difficult one for Kerala state. In addition, remittance losses were put at $180 million.

If the specific impact of the Gulf crisis due to loss of migrant workers' jobs and remittances is difficult enough to estimate, assessment of the more general impact on Asian economies is even more difficult. Its immediate effect was a sharp increase in the price of oil, but increases in output by other producers, along with other factors, fairly soon resulted in a fall in prices, virtually to pre-crisis levels. Nevertheless, high oil prices in the second half of 1990 caused problems for several economies in the region. The overall impact of the crisis is estimated by the Asian Development Bank at between 1.5 and 3 per cent of GDP for Bangladesh and Sri Lanka, and 0.5 per cent for India,[1] with Pakistan and the Philippines also

---

1. The Indian government has made a careful calculation of the direct impact of the Gulf crisis on its balance of payments. The Economic Survey for 1990–91 puts this at Rs 51,800 million, or around $ 2,900 million at 1990 exchange rates, equivalent to 36 per cent of the year's balance-of-payments deficit. Of this cost, 70 per cent is accounted for by additional net spending on oil imports, 10 per cent by the loss of export markets in West Asia, 4 per cent by the non-realisation of other export dues from Iraq, 9 per cent by loss of remittances from Iraq and Kuwait, and 7 per cent by the foreign exchange costs of emergency repatriation.

'adversely affected'. Initial economic imbalances exacerbated the effect of the crisis in some countries, such as India and the Philippines, with large and widening budget and balance-of-payments deficits, strong inflationary pressures, low levels of foreign exchange reserves and high debt service ratios.

Thus, in general, the problems for Asian labour markets arising from the need to absorb workers who would otherwise have migrated to Kuwait and Iraq, and to reabsorb those who were displaced, were aggravated by the (quantitatively, probably much more important) fall in demand for labour arising from falls in remittances and in earnings from exports and tourism, and from slower growth due to higher oil prices. However, the early end to the Gulf war opened the way for resumption of normal trade and migrant flows from mid-1991 onwards.

1.3   Recent Trends in the Employment and Labour Market Situation

Recent trends in the region's labour markets reflect the economic trends discussed in the first two sections.

In the newly industrialising economies, even though growth has slowed, labour markets have continued to be tight. In particular, there is a shortage of unskilled and semi-skilled workers to do the dirty, demanding and dangerous (widely known as '3-D') jobs increasingly avoided by indigenous workers. This has given rise to a debate about the import of foreign labour into the NIEs, and to an increasing use of such workers, often on an illegal basis.[1]

In Hong Kong,[2] shortages, particularly of professionals, managers and skilled workers, are related to emigration, estimated at around 62,000 in 1990, in anticipation of the reversion of Hong Kong to China due in 1997. There is no problem in principle in importing workers in these categories (although it is unlikely to be possible on the scale needed—only 6,200 arrived in 1989). The issue of importing unskilled and semi-skilled workers, of whom there is also an acute shortage, is much more contentious. The government decision in 1990 to allow an additional 12,000 foreign semi-skilled workers to join the work force (in the garment industry, export-import trades, retailing and hotels and tourism) was greeted with an outcry from trade unions.

In the Republic of Korea, although some small businesses are reported to have approached the government about the possibility of importing foreign workers (and high Korean wages are a potent attraction), illegal immigration is not yet an important phenomenon. Nevertheless, Korean labour markets are very tight, particularly in the construction sector, where wage increases reached 21 per cent in 1989 and 17 per cent in 1990. Labour-intensive industries, such as textiles, footwear and garments, are officially estimated to be short of 20 to 30 per cent of the work force that they need, and bus and taxi companies have 11 per cent of their vehicles off the road because of lack of drivers.[3] The migration of young people to urban areas is also reported to be causing labour shortages in some rural areas in the planting and harvesting seasons.

---

1.   See US Department of Labour (1991), on which our discussion of labour shortages draws heavily.
2.   See Mohanty (1991) for further discussion.
3.   *National Herald*, New Delhi, 11 July 1991.

In Singapore the government has been trying to reduce reliance on foreign workers in recent years. In 1989 it increased the penalties both for illegal aliens and for those employing them. As an unexpected consequence, thousands of foreign construction workers (particularly from Thailand and India) volunteered for repatriation, bringing several important construction projects to a halt. Since then the government has streamlined procedures for the legal admission of foreign workers, and allowed married working women who employ a foreign maid to claim an income tax rebate, but it has also increased the monthly levy payable by employers on foreign workers to twice its 1988 level and reduced the ceiling on the proportion of such workers that can be employed by a company from 50 to 40 per cent. Meanwhile its shortages of unskilled and semi-skilled labour have become even more pronounced.

In Taiwan–China the import of illegal foreign workers for 3-D jobs has been going on for years, and the number in residence is variously estimated at between 20,000 and 140,000. In 1990 an attempt was made to curb the entry of illegal workers and to provide a legal channel for the employment of foreigners in major public construction projects. However, since the wages laid down are comparable to those paid to local workers, and contractors are required to supply return air tickets and pay other expenses, this has not proved attractive to employers. Meanwhile shortages of labour persist, in the fishing industry and manufacturing as well as construction, and labour costs continue to rise. Booming labour markets, particularly in the services sector, are attracting graduates (in liberal arts as well as technical subjects) who have studied overseas back to Taiwan.

The dilemma for the NIEs considering the question of labour imports is the same as that faced by any economy running into labour shortage. It is exemplified by the argument between employers and unions in Hong Kong (Mohanty, 1991:6). Employers claim that the import of unskilled and semi-skilled labour will help overcome the labour-supply constraint on growth, ease wage-push inflation and help build badly needed infrastructure. The unions, worried about the impact of cheap imported labour on wages and bargaining power, argue that Hong Kong should restructure towards higher-technology, higher-value-added products, and that the import of cheap labour postpones this restructuring. To some extent, there is a conflict of interest on this issue between labour in low-wage and high-wage countries, although this is mitigated if restructuring involves relocation of labour-intensive operations.

Labour shortages are beginning to emerge, also, in some South East Asian economies, particularly those on the track to become the next generation of NIEs.

Malaysia is in this category, with shortages of technical, semi-skilled and unskilled workers in rubber and oil palm plantations and the construction sector, and at least half a million foreign workers in its work force, mainly from Indonesia and the Philippines. As a short-term measure, the prime minister announced in July 1991[1] that the intake of foreign labour will be increased. At the same time, while the comparatively high unemployment rate can probably be attributed to definitional differences, unemployment is a problem among educated first-job-seekers and in tin-mining areas.

---

1. *International Herald Tribune*, 11 July 1991.

Thailand, also, is in transition from labour surplus to labour shortage. The benefits to labour of faster growth are more evident in urban than in rural areas (the north-east, in particular, remains depressed), but markets for unskilled workers are becoming tighter and there are shortages of skilled-and-above workers, especially in engineering and management. There are worries about a lack of response of the educational system to the changing pattern of demand in industry; at 28 per cent, Thailand's secondary enrolment rate is the lowest in South East Asia.

Indonesia is at an early stage in the journey towards NIE status, but recent rapid growth has certainly boosted the demand for labour. Export manufacturing has been a leading sector in this process, with the dollar value of such exports growing at an annual average rate of nearly 43 per cent between 1983 and 1990. This has not only generated more than a million extra jobs in manufacturing, but also, more important, contributed to growth of employment in other sectors which supply inputs to the manufacturing sector, produce wage goods and services for its employees, and provide banking, financial, transport and marketing services. Expansion of the financial sector since its deregulation in December 1988 has generated heavy excess demand for professionals and semi-professionals in this field, partly met by converting those qualified in other specialisations (such as architecture and engineering).

Other South East Asian economies are, for one reason or another, still far from enjoying a shortage of labour. In the Philippines political instability and lack of progress in structural reforms has meant weak growth in demand for labour in all sectors during 1990 and continued reliance on export of labour (with the number of contract workers overseas estimated at around two million in 1991). The relative increase in employment in the services sector in 1990 signifies lack of alternatives rather than a positive change in structure (Ofreneo, 1991). Vietnam's enormous potential is shown by the response of its agricultural, trade and services sectors to recent reforms. But current employment problems are serious, aggravated by demobilisation of members of the armed forces and the return of migrant workers, from Eastern Europe as well as from Iraq.

South Asia, also, is still in the early stages of the journey towards labour shortage, although there are promising signs in some countries.

It is difficult to assess what is going on in India's labour markets. Slow growth in employment in the organised sector, particularly in manufacturing, has meant that most of the increase in labour force during the 1980s has had to be absorbed by the unorganised sector, particularly into construction.[1] A sign of avoidance of labour regulations, also, is the increase in the relative importance of casual wage employment; among urban male workers the proportion of casual wage employees rose from 13 to 15 per cent over the ten years to 1988, at the expense of regular salaried employment which fell from 46 to 43 per cent. The crucial question concerns the nature of these new types of employment that are expanding relatively fast—are they a sign of the dynamism of flexible labour markets, or of distress on the part of workers in markets that appear increasingly to be loaded against them?

---

1. See Planning Commission (1990) for further discussion.

Trends in Pakistan are easier to detect.[1] In contrast to the 1970s and early 1980s, when a large net outflow of workers to West Asia reduced labour supply and a huge inflow of remittances boosted demand, more recently (with net return migration for several years before the Gulf crisis) labour markets have returned to a more normal state of oversupply. Real wages of construction workers, which increased by more than 50 per cent in the second half of the 1970s, have stopped rising. As in India there has been a trend towards casualisation of wage labour, and the organised sector is absorbing very few additional workers.

Bangladesh scarcely had time to absorb the impact of the Gulf crisis before it was hit by an even worse disaster—the cyclone of April 1991. This put paid to hopes of continuing the progress shown in 1990, when Bangladesh was the fastest-growing economy in South Asia. Even that had not done much to improve the situation in the labour market—real wages, which have stagnated for years, are estimated to have increased only marginally in 1990.

In Sri Lanka a revival in labour-intensive exports and tourism has increased demand for labour, offsetting to some extent the effects of the Gulf crisis. However, unemployment of educated first-job-seekers remains an apparently chronic problem.

Fluctuations in the rate of growth of demand for labour have remained a major problem in the Pacific Islands. In Fiji employment, having grown by 13 per cent in 1989, rose by only 1 per cent in 1990, a bad year for its labour-intensive export industries in particular. In Papua New Guinea a sharp fall in employment in the mining sector in 1989 was offset by a 3 per cent increase in employment in other parts of the organised sector; but in 1990 most sectors experienced a decline in employment.

Finally, the recent easing of the hectic pace of growth in China has meant a deterioration in the underlying employment situation, but not in a visible way. The postponement of new urban construction projects has resulted in the return of many construction workers to rural areas, and the rate of urban unemployment has actually fallen. The recession in industry is reflected in even more on-the-job underemployment, but the still rigid labour market and the absence of a social security system have limited the amount of retrenchment that has occurred.

It is one thing, thus, to describe the trends in employment and labour market situation in the various countries in the region and quite another to provide a comparable, quantitative measure of those trends. Table 2 summarises some of the data that are often used for this purpose.

High population density in all the countries represented in the Table except Malaysia, Myanmar and Fiji, though variably offset by non-labour inputs,[2] creates a presumption that at least some of them could still be described as labour-surplus. But the main impression gained from the Table is of the inadequacy of these kinds of labour-force data for measuring the scale of a country's employment problem, and, even more, for monitoring changes in its extent over time.

The difficulties begin with the concept of unemployment. In all the countries in the Table except three the unemployment rate is low—3 per cent or less. The three exceptions are Malaysia, the Philippines and Fiji. Does this mean that these

---

1. See ILO-ARTEP (1991a:16-28) for further discussion.
2. See Mahmood (1991) for further discussion.

three countries have a worse employment problem than others in the region? The answer is 'no'. They are merely using a different measure. In the majority of cases. a strict definition of active or open unemployment (both 'not working' and 'seeking work') is being used. In countries without social security systems, where few (and those mainly educated first-job-seekers) can afford the luxury of a full-time job search, this inevitably means a low unemployment rate, relatively insensitive to changes in labour market conditions. For instance, the unemployment rate in Taiwan-China increased in 1990, even though the labour market was getting tighter. And the rate in Indonesia has remained steady for over a decade at 3 per cent or less, in spite of presumable upswings and downswings in the demand for labour as the oil boom in the first half of the 1980s was followed by recession.

If the unemployment rate is insensitive to changes in market conditions, this undermines the usefulness of the quantity of employment as an indicator. In particular, it means that it makes little sense to compare the rates of growth of employment, on the one hand, and the labour force, on the other, shown in Table 2. The quantity of employment, defined as the labour force minus the unemployed, is supply-determined in such an economy. An increase in the labour force will automatically be reflected in an increase in 'employment', but how much of this employment is real and how much is merely a refuge for job-seekers in distress remains undiscoverable from the statistics. A stagnant economy with a high rate of labour force growth and a dynamic economy with a booming demand for labour may well both have a similar rate of increase in 'employment'. This renders an employment-elasticity approach to planning and evaluation largely meaningless.

One way of trying to get round this problem is to devise a more useful definition of underutilisation of labour. This, in effect, is what the three countries with higher unemployment rates in Table 2 have tried to do. It usually involves relaxing the 'seeking-work' and/or the 'not-working' criteria, to give measures of various kinds of unemployment or underemployment. However, all are problematic in one way or another, particularly if it is hoped to use them as a guide to changes over time.

Relaxation of the seeking-work criterion yields the concept of the 'inactively unemployed', not working, not seeking work but available for work. The practical difficulty here is in defining availability for work in a precise, unambiguous and surveyable way. After all, anyone's availability for work will tend to depend on the kind of work in question, its location and level of remuneration; it cannot be defined in the abstract.

Relaxation of the not-working criterion takes us in the direction of underemployment. Anyone working fewer than normal hours while actively seeking additional work could be described as suffering from active visible underemployment; and, if the seeking-work criterion were also relaxed, part-time workers not seeking but available for extra work could presumably be described as the inactive visibly underemployed. Care has to be taken with this concept, however, as the huge estimates of visible underemployment current in some developing countries (for instance, 33 per cent in Bangladesh in 1988, 40 per cent in Indonesia in 1986, 37 per cent in the Philippines in July 1990) often include many who are voluntarily working fewer than normal hours.

TABLE 2
Labour Force, Employment and Unemployment in Selected Asian Countries

	Population density per sq. km. 1989	Labour force (mn) 1989	Labour force ann. avg. growth rate 1988 and 1989	Employment ann. avg. growth rate 1988 and 1989	Unemployment Rate		
					1988	1989	1990
Newly Industrialising Economies							
Hong Kong	5424	2.8	0.7%	1.1%	1.4%	1.1%	1.6%
Korea, Rep.	428	18.0	3.2%	3.5%	2.5%	2.6%	—
Singapore	4367	1.3	2.1%	1.6%	3.4%	2.1%	2.0%
Taiwan–China	556	8.4	1.3%	1.5%	1.7%	1.6%	2.4%
South East Asia							
Indonesia	94	74.5*	3.1%*	3.0%*	2.6%	—	—
Malaysia	53	6.8	1.7%	1.7%	8.1%	7.1%	6.0%
Philippines	200	23.9	2.4%	2.4%	8.3%	8.6%	9.0%
Thailand	108	30.5*	6.6%*	6.6%*	3.0%	—	—
South Asia							
Bangladesh	758	30.4#	3.3%#	3.0%#	—	—	—
India	247	—	—	1.2%*	—	—	—
Myanmar	59	15.6**	-1.1%**	-0.1%**	1.4%**	—	—
Pakistan	137	30.1**	2.6%**	3.3%**	3.1%**	—	—
Sri Lanka	255	5.9@	—	—	—	—	—
China, People's Rep.	116	550.6	1.8%	1.8%	2.0%	2.0%	—
Pacific Islands							
Fiji	40	0.3	0.9%	7.0%	10.3%	8.9%	6.4%

Notes: — not available.
* 1988 only. ** 1987 only. # 1986 only. @ 1985 only.

Sources: Key Indicators of Developing Asian and Pacific Countries, Asian Development Bank, July 1990. *World Development Report*, World Bank, 1991.

Even trickier is the concept of invisible underemployment, which involves relaxing the not-working criterion altogether, while retaining the seeking-work criterion to cover those working a full normal week while desperately looking for a 'real' job. So much so that labour statisticians have described it as 'primarily an analytical concept' not amenable to statistical measurement (Resolution of the Thirteenth International Conference of Labour Statisticians, Geneva, 1982).

All in all, these expanded concepts of unemployment and underemployment are far too subtle to be captured by regular, routine surveys in such a way as to illuminate trends in underutilisation of labour over time. In particular, they demand great skill from enumerators in interpreting the definitions to respondents and ensuring their consistency between surveys. Thus, a labour-force approach to the analysis of a country's employment problem can throw some light on the nature and structure of that problem at a point in time, but can usually tell us very little about how it is changing from year to year.

1.4   Alternative Indicators of Changes in the Labour Market Situation

Fortunately another indicator of changes in the employment situation is available which is not only cheaper to collect but also potentially much more revealing of overall trends. Wage rates in those parts of the labour market to which entry is relatively easy (demanding little in the way of capital and skills) and competitive should be sensitive to changes in most of the types of underutilisation discussed above. The loss of income from work entailed in unemployment and visible underemployment will tend to lower the supply price of those who do not have other compensating sources of income. Their availability for work and that of the invisibly underemployed will exert downward pressures on real wages. Thus one indicator can in principle encapsulate the impact of a number of changes in the labour market which are complex and otherwise difficult to measure.

Although in most of developing Asia the self-employed are more numerous than wage earners, the real wage rate is preferred to the earnings of the self-employed, as an indicator, on grounds of collectability. Problems of isolating the returns to labour and of ensuring a comparable sample over time mean that a regular survey of the earnings of the self-employed would be too management-intensive to become a routine part of the programme of a government statistical agency.

In any case, concentration on what is happening in the wage-employing sector is not necessarily a misleading guide to the state of labour markets even in economies where wage employment is still relatively small. This, after all, was the focus of Lewis' classical model of an economy with unlimited supplies of labour (Lewis, 1954), which offers a useful (and so far neglected) framework for quantification in this field.

It must be admitted that there is a long way to go before reliable and comparable series of wage statistics are available for every country in the region. Even for the manufacturing sector alone, only eight countries make wage data widely available, and these are of varying reliability, specification and timeliness. Tables 3 and 4 show recent trends in manufacturing real wages in these economies, deflated first by consumer prices and secondly by producer prices.[1]

TABLE 3

Index of Real Wages in Manufacturing, Deflated by Consumer Prices, Selected Asian Economies, 1985–90

	1985	1986	1987	1988	1989	1990
China, PR*	100	107	109	114	110	—
Hong Kong#	100	105	112	119	124	129
India*	100	100	100	101	100	—
Indonesia@	100	93	94	92	—	—
Korea, Rep.*	100	106	115	129	152	—
Philippines#	100	99	101	112	—	—
Singapore*	100	97	102	108	115	—
Sri Lanka@	100	99	100	98	—	—

Notes: * earnings per month
rate per day
@ earnings per day
In the case of China, sector includes mining, quarrying, electricity, gas and water, as well as manufacturing.
— not available

Sources: Wages: *Yearbook of Labour Statistics* and *Bulletin of Labour Statistics*, ILO; *Indian Labour Journal*, Labour Bureau, Ministry of Labour, Government of India; *Survei Upah Buruh*, Biro Pusat Statistik, Jakarta, Indonesia. Prices: Implicit GDP deflators for manufacturing sector from Asian Development Bank, *Key Indicators of Developing Asian and Pacific Countries*, July 1990 (except India: wholesale price index for manufacturing from *Economic Survey 1989-90*, Government of India).

TABLE 4

Index of Real Wages in Manufacturing, Deflated by Producer Prices, Selected Asian Economies, 1985–89

	1985	1986	1987	1988	1989
China, PR*	100	111	114	127	133
Hong Kong#	100	105	110	115	119
India*	100	105	109	108	107
Indonesia@	100	97	96	95	—
Korea, Rep.*	100	107	120	137	166
Philippines#	100	98	99	109	—
Singapore*	100	93	97	100	109
Sri Lanka@	100	102	103	102	—

Notes: * earnings per month
rate per day
@ earnings per day.
— not available.

Sources: Wages: as for Table 3. Prices: *Asian Development Outlook*, Asian Development Bank, 1991.

---

1. The index of producer prices is approximated by that of the implicit GDP deflators for the manufacturing sector.

As can be seen, in spite of the fact that the wage series in all except two cases[1] are from a single international source, three different definitions are represented in the Tables, and in three cases no information more recent than 1988 are available. There must be doubts, also, about the quality of these little-used data. Nevertheless they can be used to illustrate an alternative approach to labour market analysis, in which the focus is on changes over time rather than on levels.

For ease of inspection, in the case of six of the countries in Tables 3 and 4, the trends in the two types of real wage are shown in a graph in Figures 1 and 2.

As far as recent real manufacturing wage trends seen from the point of view of workers are concerned, as in Table 3 and Figure 1, the countries of the region fall into three groups. In some they have been upward—strongly in the case of Korea, less so in the case of Hong Kong, even less so in the cases of Singapore, China and the Philippines. This is a mixed group of economies. Significantly, it includes all the presumably labour-shortage NIEs for which data are available, as well as two economies which are far from labour shortage—one (China) undergoing a slow and painful process of labour market reform, the other (the Philippines) grappling with a wide range of political and social problems. The second group, with a more or less constant real wage over the period, consists of the two South Asian countries in Table 3, India and Sri Lanka. The third group, of one, is Indonesia, the only country with a significant downward trend in real manufacturing wages in the second half of the 1980s.

Looked at from the point of view of employers, as in Table 4 and Figure 2, real wage trends are not much different, except in the cases of Singapore and India. In Singapore, particularly in 1985–88, wage-earners and employers had the best of both worlds. Wage earners enjoyed rising real wages, deflated by consumer prices, while employers (because industrial prices were rising faster than consumer prices) enjoyed constant real wages, deflated by producer prices. In India it was the other way round. Because industrial prices were rising more slowly than consumer prices, wage-earners enjoyed no increase in real wages, but employers were faced with a rising trend. This is a useful illustration of the distinction between real consumer wages and real producer wages. The former are of interest when the focus is on the welfare of wage-earners, but real producer wages are more relevant to analysis of labour markets, as will emerge below.

Inspection of trends in real wages alone is not, however, enough for labour market analysis. Several other variables need to be incorporated. The most important of these is the *number of wage employees*. Here again achievements in data collection and publication leave much to be desired.

Table 5 shows trends in paid employment in manufacturing in the same eight economies, which, between them, manage seven different definitions of the variable; in only half the cases are the data confined to the wage employees strictly relevant to our analysis, and again, in many cases the series are of historical rather than current interest. As can be seen, the trend in this period is generally upward, with the exceptions of India (where the statistics reflect the stagnation of the organised

---

1. The two exceptions are India and Indonesia. For India the data are unweighted average monthly earnings of lowest paid workers in the cotton textile industry; for Indonesia unweighted average daily earnings of production workers in manufacturing.

FIGURE 1

Trends in Manufacturing Real Wages, Deflated by Consumer Prices

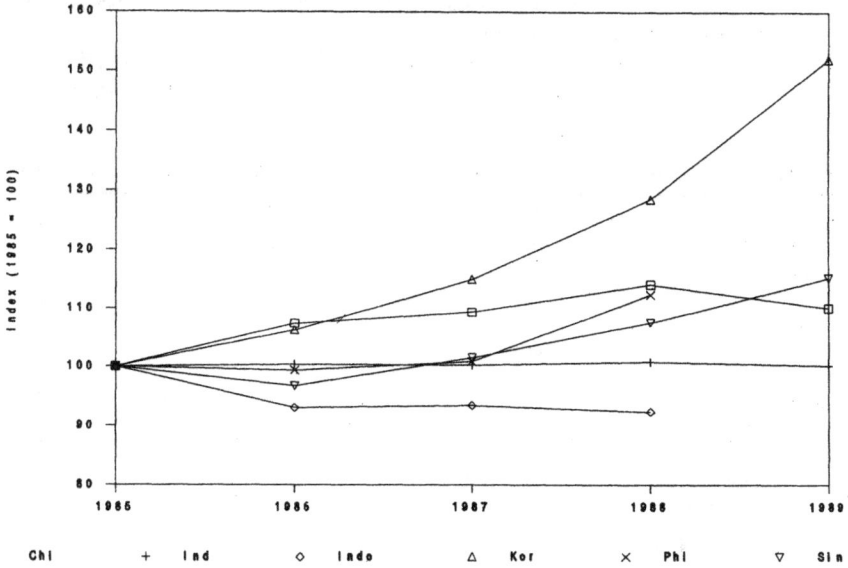

Chi + Ind ◇ Indo △ Kor × Phi ▽ Sin

FIGURE 2

Trends in Manufacturing Real Wages, Deflated by Producer Prices

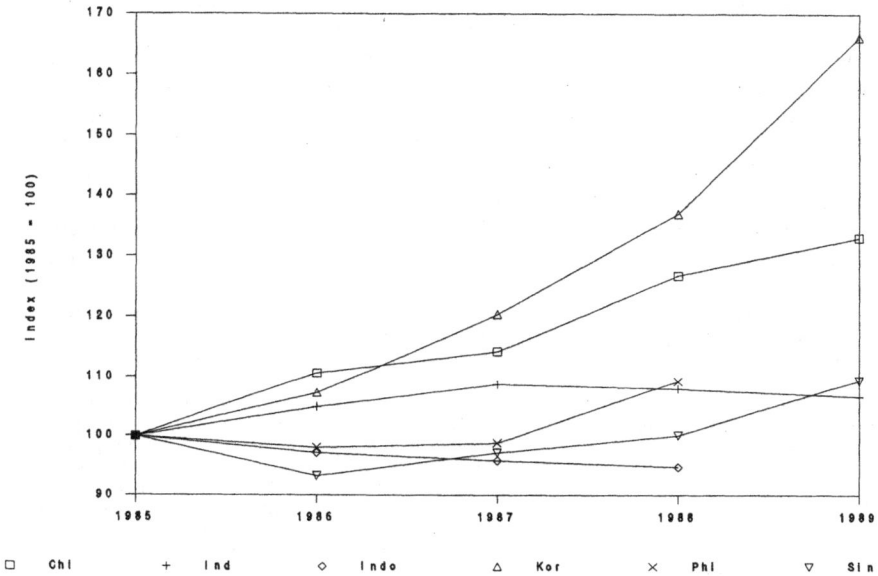

□ Chi + Ind ◇ Indo △ Kor × Phi ▽ Sin

sector) and Hong Kong (where a structural shift towards the services sector has occurred.)

A third variable to be incorporated into the analysis is *value added per worker* in manufacturing, obtained by dividing an index of value added in the sector (at constant prices) by the index of paid employment, and shown in Table 6. Hong Kong drops out of this table because of the absence of data on value added in manufacturing.

TABLE 5

Trends in Paid Employment in Manufacturing, Selected Asian Economies, 1985–1990

	1985	1986	1987	1988	1989
China, PR*	100	104	107	111	117
Hong Kong#	100	102	102	99	93
India+	100	101	101	101	—
Indonesia¥	100	100	101	107	—
Korea, Rep.§	100	106	123	129	139
Philippines@	100	99	107	113	120
Singapore¶	100	98	109	122	128
Sri Lanka§	100	106	—	—	—

Notes: — not available
* employees in state-owned enterprises,
# all persons engaged
+ Employees and working proprietors, public sector and 10+ private sector.
¥ all persons engaged in 20+ establishments
§ employees in 5+ establishments
@ employees
¶ all persons engaged in private 10+ establishments.
Sources: *Yearbook of Labour Statistics* and *Bulletin of Labour Statistics*, ILO.

The data on real wages (deflated by producer prices), paid employment and value added per worker in manufacturing can be combined in a single diagram for each of the six countries with series of four years or more, as in Figures 3 to 8. These give a picture of how the manufacturing labour market has looked to employers in each of the countries in recent years. Together with qualitative information on what is going on in these labour markets, they should enable us to put each of them into a broad category—for instance, labour-shortage/competitive, labour-shortage/segmented,[1] labour-surplus/competitive, labour-surplus/segmented.[2]

In only two cases, Korea and the Philippines (Figures 3 and 4), and for very different reasons, have real wages tended to rise faster than value added per worker

---

1.   A segmented labour market is one in which workers with otherwise similar individual characteristics (age, education, labour market experience, etc.) earn different amounts because they differ in one or more respect (gender, ethnic group, sector in which they work, size/type of firm for which they work, etc.)

2.   What are the defining characteristics of a labour-surplus economy? In his pioneering paper Lewis (1954) attributed unlimited supplies of labour to an economy in which employers in the capitalist sector are faced with a perfectly elastic supply curve of labour (as a function of the producer wage, measured in units of output of the capitalist sector). However, as attempts to make the Lewis model more rigorous (e.g., Ranis and Fei, 1961) showed, the arithmetic of labour transfer is such that special assumptions are necessary to preserve the possibility of a perfectly horizontal labour supply curve, even where there is surplus labour in the subsistence sector, potentially available for employment at the going wage. This means that we should be fairly relaxed in allowing an economy with fluctuations in the supply-price of labour, as demand for labour increases, still to be defined as a labour-surplus economy, as long as those fluctuations are not occurring around a steeply rising trend.

FIGURE 3

Real Wage, Value Added per Worker and Employment, Manufacturing, Korea, 1985–89

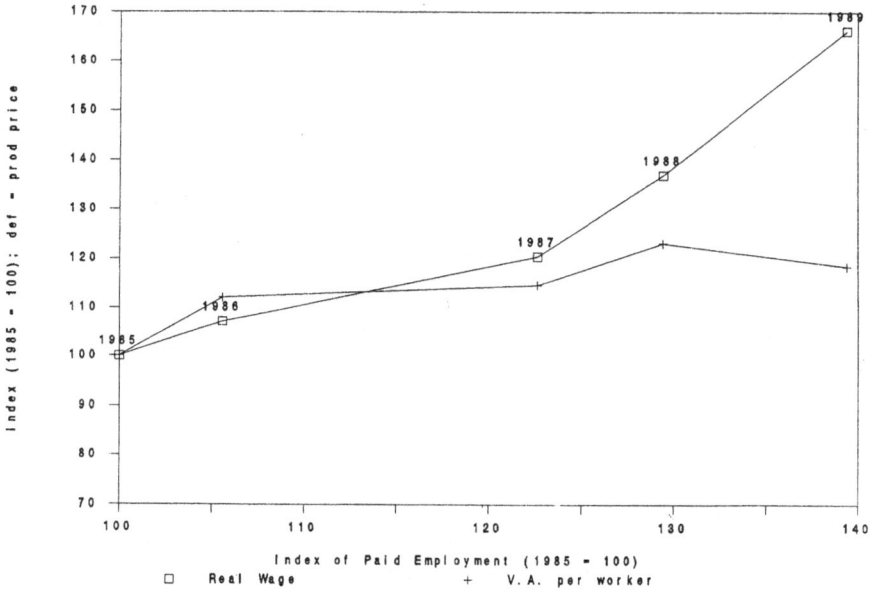

FIGURE 4

Real Wage, Value Added per Worker and Employment, Manufacturing, Philippines, 1985–88

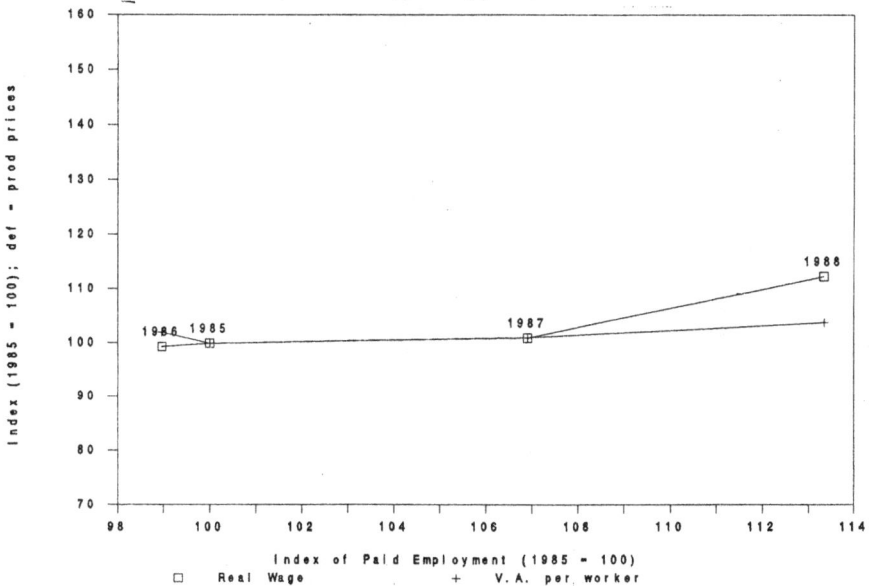

FIGURE 5

Real Wage, Value Added per Worker and Employment, Manufacturing, Singapore, 1985–89

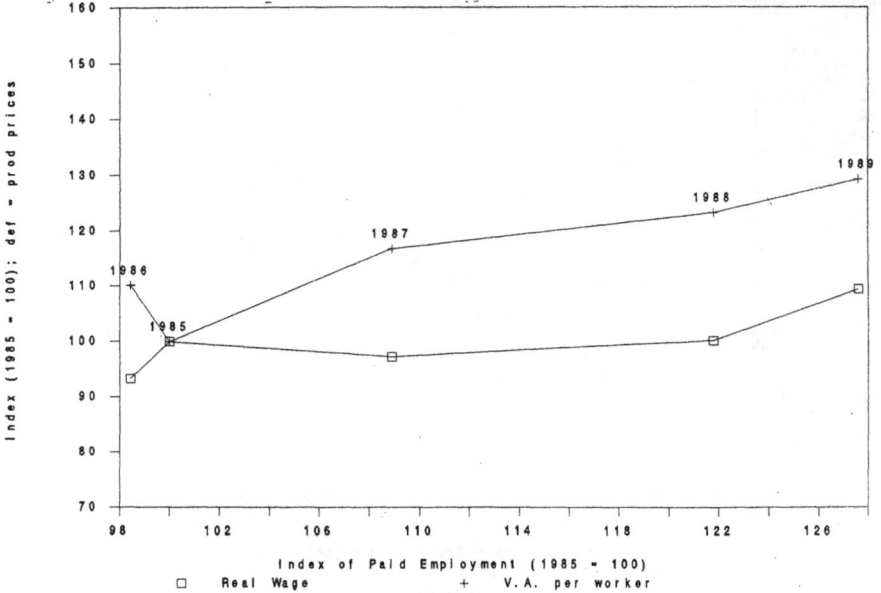

FIGURE 6

Real Wage, Value Added per Worker and Employment, Manufacturing, China, 1985–89

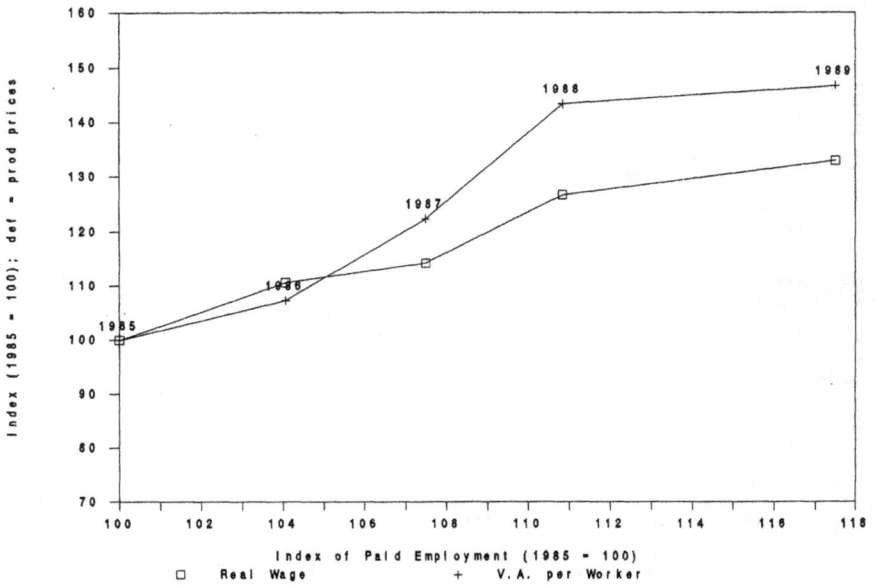

FIGURE 7

Real Wage, Value Added per Worker and Employment, Manufacturing, India, 1985–88

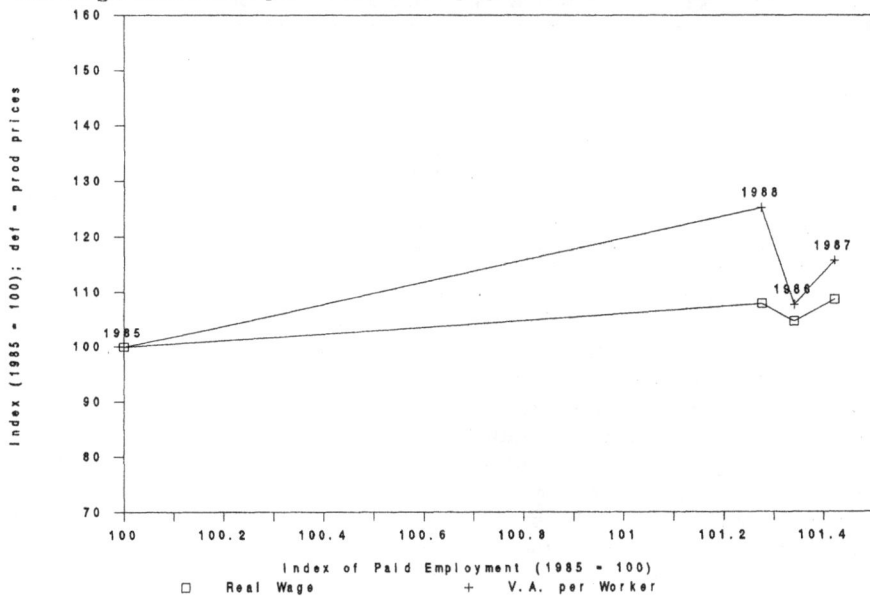

FIGURE 8

Real Wage, Value Added per Worker and Employment, Manufacturing, Indonesia, 1985–88

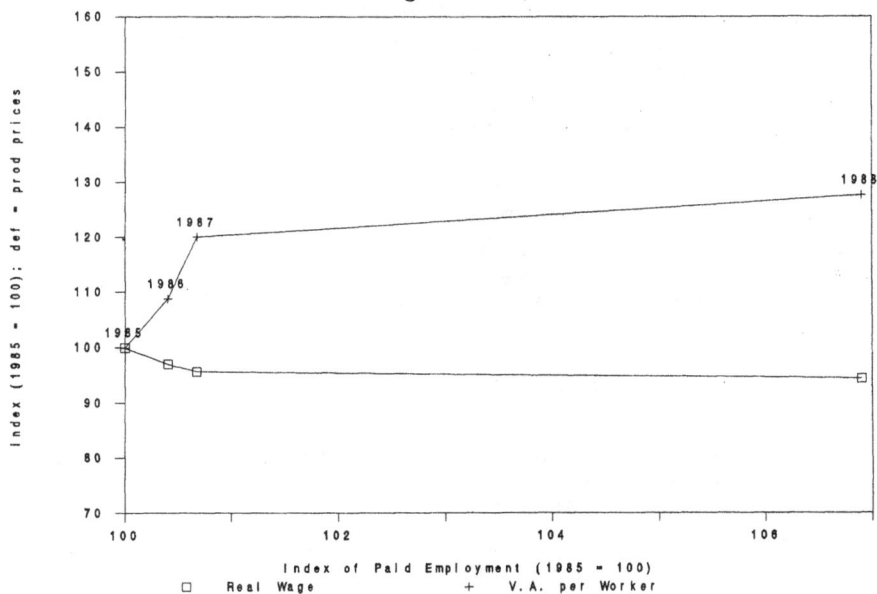

TABLE 6

Trends in Value Added per Worker in Manufacturing, Selected Asian Economics, 1985–89

	1985	*1986*	*1987*	*1988*	*1989*
China, PR	100	107	122	143	147
India	100	108	116	125	—
Indonesia	100	109	120	128	—
Korea, Rep.	100	112	115	123	118
Philippines	100	102	101	104	104
Singapore	100	110	117	123	129
Sri Lanka	100	100	—	—	—

Note: — not available.
Source: Asian Development Bank (1991) Table A4 and Table 5.

as employment has increased. In the dynamic Korean context this reflects claims by labour for a greater share of the product, after years of fast productivity growth. In the relatively stagnant Philippines, it reflects the power of labour to secure a real wage increase even when value added per worker is hardly rising.

In Singapore (Figure 5), unlike Korea, value added per worker is still rising faster than real wages as employment increases. The same is true in China (Figure 6), which is prematurely behaving like an NIE. Rigidities in its still over-supplied labour market have meant rising wages as employment has expanded, but value added per worker has risen even faster. In India (Figure 7), as employment in the organised manufacturing sector inches painfully upward, real producer wages also rise, but not as fast as value added per worker.

Indonesia's is the case most favourable to employers, to judge from Figure 8, with a steep increase in value added per worker (particularly in 1985–87) accompanying expansion of employment and a slight fall in real wages.

Categorisation of these labour markets, on the basis of Figures 3 to 8, if the data can be believed, and of other information, is not too difficult. Singapore (Figure 5) appears to have a competitive market, with wages rising because of shortage of labour rather than union power. Korea (Figure 3), on the other hand, appears to be running into political/institutional difficulties, with wages rising faster than productivity, and could be categorised as labour-shortage/segmented. The other economies appear still to have surplus labour. India (Figure 7) is difficult to classify because of the tiny increase in manufacturing employment, but its labour market may not be as segmented as is generally assumed. The labour markets of the Philippines (Figure 4) and China (Figure 6) may, in their different ways, be described as segmented, while Indonesia's (Figure 8) is clearly competitive.

Data problems aside,[1] it is hoped that enough has been done to show how much more revealing of labour market situations and of changes over time is analysis of

---

1. There are, admittedly, many headaches in defining and measuring the real wage. There are problems of standardising the definition of the nominal wage, to include or to exclude (in addition to the basic wage) allowances, payments in kind, fringe benefits, etc.. The calculation of the deflator also raises problems, though probably fewer if the interest, as in this case, is in the producer price rather than the consumer price index. Nevertheless, the real wage raises far fewer conceptual problems than do most direct measures of labour underutilisation, and looks more amenable to improvement and analysis.

real wages, wage employment and value added per worker than is analysis of the usual measures of underutilisation of labour as revealed by labour force surveys. In particular, it represents perhaps the only way of checking whether surplus labour still exists in an economy. Moreover, the issues it raises are not of mere academic interest but relevant to policy. For instance, it shows that competitive and 'efficient' labour markets (Indonesia) with low rates of unemployment and underemployment, as measured by traditional labour force methods, can still have concealed surplus labour available for employment, should demand increase, without much rise in real wages. This raises the possibility of expanding demand for labour in such economies without necessarily any danger of causing runaway inflation. Alternatively, in cases where wages are rising for reasons other than or in addition to the emergence of labour shortage (China), and particularly where they are rising faster than value added per worker (Korea, the Philippines), it draws attention to the need for policy to address this problem.

For employment planners and statisticians this discussion of alternative indicators raises some practical issues. It suggests the possibility of carrying out (complex and expensive) labour force surveys much less frequently than has become common, for occasional benchmark purposes, and using analysis of the kind of data discussed in this section to track trends. This poses the challenge to planners of putting wage, price, wage employment and value added statistics in order. A common definition needs to be adopted, for comparative purposes, at least throughout Asia, of wage and wage employment. New, cheap and simple surveys need to be designed, so that policy-makers can have access to the data, not just for one but for all sectors, and not as now of three years ago, but of last month.[1]

1.5 Policy Issues

The trend in policy-making throughout the region is clear. Governments are, almost without exception, trying to 'get prices right' and to remove institutional obstacles to the better working of markets and to the achievement of international competitiveness.

They are doing this with varying success, as a review of recent policy implementation shows.

1.5.1 Getting Prices Right

Many economists see factor price distortions as a sufficient explanation of unemployment and underemployment. They point, in particular, to overvalued exchange rates, low interest rates and 'high' wages. Overvaluation of the exchange rate, they suggest, encourages imports of capital goods and discourages the use of domestic labour-intensive inputs. Low interest rates mean that credit is rationed rather than allocated by price and a capital-intensive bias is imparted to choice of technology or output; private savings are also discouraged. And high wages (reflecting trade union pressure or minimum wage regulations) limit the extent of labour absorption in the high-wage sector.

---

1. This set of indicators (or as many of them as can be collected in a timely way) could come to play a role similar to that of the unemployment rate in an economy with a social security system, usually available to policy-makers and the press within a few weeks.

TABLE 7

Real Interest Rate (Lending), Selected Asian Economies, 1984–89

(Percentage)

	1984	*1985*	*1986*	*1987*	*1988*	*1989*
Newly Industrialising Economies						
Korea, Republic	7.7	7.5	7.2	7.0	2.9	5.7
Singapore	6.4	7.4	8.2	5.6	4.4	3.8
South East Asia						
Indonesia			15.7	12.4	14.1	15.2
Malaysia	7.4	11.2	10.1	7.3	5.3	4.2
Philippines	−22.2	5.5	16.7	9.6	7.2	8.6
Thailand	17.9	16.5	15.2	12.4	11.2	9.6
South Asia						
Bangladesh	1.5	1.3	3.0	6.5	6.6	6.0
India	8.3	10.9	7.8	7.7	7.1	10.3
Nepal	14.2	8.9	−3.3	4.2	6.0	6.2
Sri Lanka	−3.4	11.9	3.6	2.1	−1.6	1.6
Pacific Islands						
Fiji	8.2	9.1	11.7	7.8	8.7	5.4
Papua New Guinea	3.3	7.8	6.8	8.6	7.3	10.1
Solomon Islands	0.9	3.3	1.5	6.3	1.3	3.1
Tonga	9.9	−6.8	−11.7	5.3	0.1	8.9
Western Samoa	8.0	9.9	13.1	12.9	9.0	10.6

Source: International Financial Statistics, IMF.

Employment planners in most Asian economies seem to go along with this argument, to judge at least from policy statements. How far their aspirations have been fulfilled, as far as interest rates are concerned, can be seen from Table 7.

Table 7 shows real rather than nominal interest rates, since this is what is relevant to the intending investor. As can be seen, most economies have managed to achieve positive real interest rates (on bank loans) most of the time. Indeed, in some countries (Indonesia, Thailand) such rates have been extraordinarily high, going far above what is useful as an incentive to greater labour intensity, with probably a net depressing effect on the demand for labour. This partly reflects these governments' commitment to maintaining an open capital account. The supply price of capital to such economies is then set by international interest rates (high over this period) plus premia for differential domestic inflation and (more important) for devaluation and other political risks. In addition, high intermediation costs have pushed up lending rates in almost all non-NIE countries. The gap between lending and deposit rates is usually very wide, and in economies with closed capital accounts depositors are offered very low real rates, negative in some cases (India, Nepal, Sri Lanka and many of the Pacific Islands, at one time or another). Thus, while positive real lending rates may predispose investors in many countries towards labour-intensive techniques (though often offset by special government low-interest lending programmes), mobilisation of savings is hindered by high-cost banking systems.

TABLE 8

Real Effective Exchange Rates, Selected Asian Economies, 1985–90

	1985	1986	1987	1988	1989	1990
Newly Industrialising Economies						
Hong Kong	100	94	92	87	92	105
Korea, Republic	100	83	83	94	109	109
Singapore	100	88	83	81	94	99
Taiwan-China	100	85	91	98	109	108
South East Asia						
Indonesia	100	76	58	56	57	57
Malaysia	100	85	81	72	69	69
Philippines	100	82	77	75	77	77
Thailand	100	88	84	79	82	86
South Asia						
Bangladesh	100	88	87	84	92	88
India	100	87	82	77	70	64
Myanmar	100	100	120	131	162	174
Nepal	100	90	88	85	79	78
Pakistan	100	82	72	72	69	67
Sri Lanka	100	91	85	84	81	85
China, People's Republic	100	74	70	80	90	70
Pacific Islands						
Fiji	100	91	78	66	66	86
Papua New Guinea	100	97	96	91	93	95
Solomon Islands	100	86	73	70	71	79
Tonga	100	102	98	107	110	111
Vanuatu	100	92	90	78	74	77
Western Samoa	100	90	84	83	82	100

Notes: * 1989 only.
Real effective exchange rate is number of dollars per unit of national currency multiplied by the national price index divided by the (weighted) trading partners' index.

Source: *Asian Development Outlook*, Asian Development Bank, 1991.

As for *exchange rates*, again it is the real rather than the nominal concept that is relevant to an evaluation. Table 8 shows how real effective exchange rates (which take into account inflation both in the country concerned and in its trading partners) have moved in recent years. For ease of inspection, the trends in six selected countries are shown graphically in Figure 9.

The main impression gained from Table 8 and Figure 9 is of virtual uniformity of achievement. All the countries represented in the Table, except for the NIEs, the special case of Myanmar and two tiny Pacific islands, had a lower real effective exchange rate (against the dollar) in 1990 than five years earlier. This means that they have not only devalued but have been able to prevent domestic wage and price rises from negating the nominal devaluation. This is true not only of the South East Asian 'success stories' but also of supposedly inflexible South Asian economies, particularly India and Pakistan. In some cases (Indonesia is the most obvious) the real effective devaluation has been so great as to raise the question of why it was

FIGURE 9

Real Effective Exchange Rates, Selected Asian Economies, 1985–90

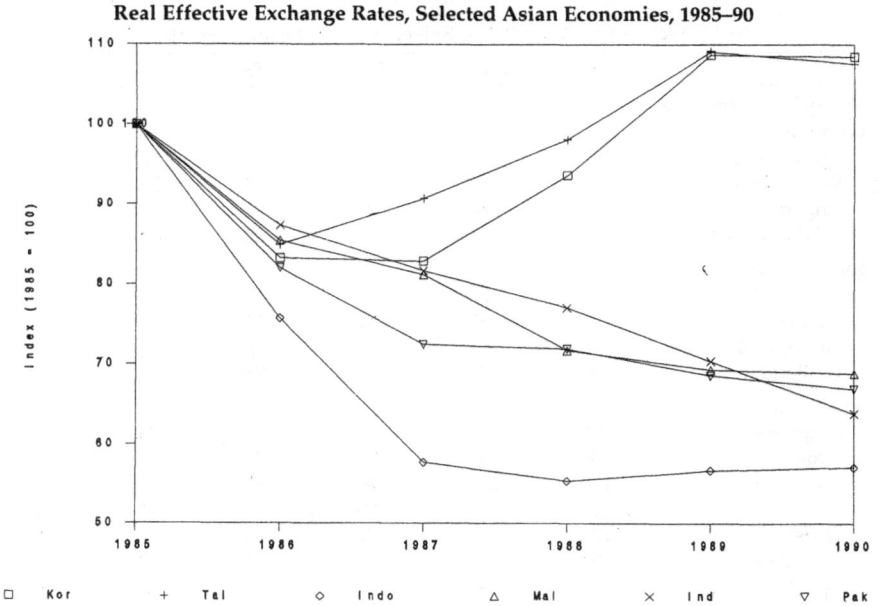

necessary on such a scale, and whether alternative, less painful measures might have been preferable.

Trends in real wages in manufacturing in eight countries were described in Table 3 and Figure 1 (deflated by consumer prices) and Table 4 and Figure 2 (deflated by producer prices). As far as the real producer wage (the most interesting concept for our purpose) is concerned, Indonesia was the only country to record a fall in the second half of the 1980s, but, apart from Korea, Hong Kong and China, increases were modest.

In these new, outward-looking models, of course, it is not enough to assess the path of real wages in local currency. They have to be converted into their dollar or yen equivalent, for comparison with trading competitors. This is done in Table 9, which shows trends in real dollar manufacturing wages in the same eight economies over the same period.

As can be seen, the combination of wage restraint and real effective devaluation has brought an improvement in international wage competitiveness to all except the NIEs and China—again spectacularly so in the case of Indonesia. But competitiveness does not depend only on relative wage levels; it also depends on what is happening to value added per worker. This finally is taken into account in Table 10 and Figure 10, which show trends in real dollar wage cost per unit of manufacturing output. Hong Kong is eliminated from the Table for lack of data on value added.

These data reveal a remarkable record. Of all the countries in Table 10 only in the case of Korea are unit wage costs higher at the end of the period than at the beginning. In the light of this, the success of Asian developing countries in world markets for labour-intensive manufactured goods is hardly surprising.

TABLE 9

Trends in Real Dollar Manufacturing Wages, Selected Asian Economies, 1985–89

(1985 = 100)

	1985	1986	1987	1988	1989
China, PR	100	82	79	101	119
Hong Kong	100	98	101	100	109
India	100	92	89	83	75
Indonesia	100	74	55	53	—
Korea, Rep.	100	89	100	128	101
Philippines	100	80	76	81	—
Singapore	100	82	81	81	103
Sri Lanka	100	93	87	85	—

Note: The real dollar wage is the real producer wage multiplied by the real effective exchange rate.
Sources: Tables 4 and 8.

TABLE 10

**Real Dollar Wage Cost per Unit of Manufacturing Output,
Selected Asian Economies, 1985–89**

	1985	1986	1987	1988	1989
China, PR	100	76	65	71	81
India	1000	85	77	66	—
Indonesia	100	68	46	41	—
Korea, Rep.	100	80	87	104	153
Philippines	100	78	75	78	—
Singapore	100	74	69	66	80
Sri Lanka	100	93	—	—	—

Note: The real dollar wage cost per unit of output is the real dollar wage divided by value added per worker.
Sources: Tables 9 and 6.

All in all, the rhetoric about factor price reform summarised at the beginning of this section certainly seems to have been followed through into practice by Asian governments. The factor price regime in most countries is now much more employment friendly than it used to be—interest rates are higher, currency values are lower, and real dollar wages and unit labour costs are lower than a few years ago. The only worry is that in some cases there seems to have been an element of overkill in price reform. The pain involved in achieving a cut in real dollar wages of 25 to 50 per cent should not be underestimated. Was all that pain really necessary to induce an expansion of investment, output, exports and employment? A tentative answer to this question will be offered at the end of the next section.

1.5.2 Institutional Reforms

The extent and pace of institutional reform has certainly been variable.[1]

Alongside exchange rate changes, there has been a general move towards the substitution of tariffs for quantitative restrictions and non-tariff barriers to interna-

---

1. This section owes much to *Asian Development Outlook*, Asian Development Bank, 1991.

FIGURE 10

Real Dollar Wage Cost per Unit of Manufacturing Output, 1985–89

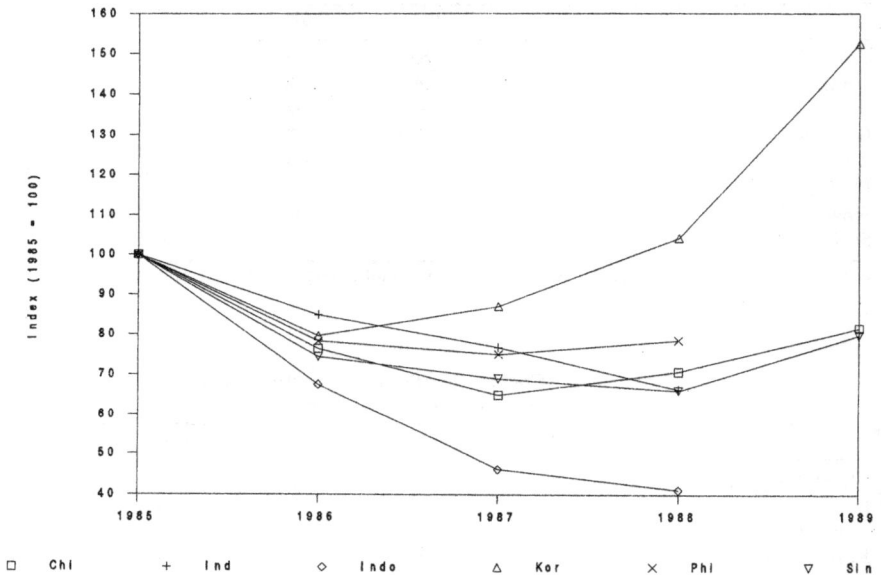

tional trade and towards lower average tariff levels. In Indonesia, for instance, the proportion of domestic production protected by quantitative restrictions fell from 41 per cent in mid-1986 to 29 per cent at the end of 1988, and by May 1990 it was estimated that 98 per cent of imports had tariffs in the zero to forty per cent range.[1] Other South East Asian countries (Malaysia, Thailand, Vietnam, but the Philippines to a lesser extent) have also been reforming their trade regimes. In general, South Asian domestic markets remain much more protected than those of East and South East Asia, with India in particular having made little progress with trade liberalisation, and with high tariffs and quantitative restrictions still affecting a large range of industrial goods in Pakistan (Kemal, 1990). China, too, although it has reduced tariffs and introduced export incentives, retains tight import restrictions.

Reforms in *industrial policy* have mostly taken the form of easing restrictions on domestic and foreign investment. In the NIEs efforts are being made to attract foreign investors into higher-value-added manufacturing with special incentives. In South East Asia, Malaysia and Thailand are making similar efforts; Indonesia has simplified licensing procedures, improved the climate for foreign investors and begun the lengthy process of reforming or privatising state enterprises; and the Philippines is lagging behind, with ambitious privatisation plans but many regula-

---

1. Jakarta Post, 29 May 1990

tions still in place. Both Vietnam and China are hesitantly grappling with the need to convert state enterprises from subsidised and centrally-directed hoarders of labour to efficient and autonomous profit-maximisers. In South Asia, Sri Lanka has had a new, liberal industrial policy since 1990, and Pakistan has taken significant steps to encourage private industrialists in general and foreign investors in particular. But perhaps the most interesting changes have occurred in India, where a radical new industrial policy was announced in July 1991, including the abolition of licensing for all industries apart from eighteen specific branches (and then for large units only), the lifting of the limit on the share of foreign investment in any enterprise from 40 to 51 per cent, automatic approval of foreign technology agreements, removal of limits on the assets of dominant enterprises in favour of a more vigorous antimonopoly policy, and the opening to the private sector of areas at present reserved for the public sector.

Labour market reform, much emphasised in the new model, is proceeding at a varying pace and often surreptitiously. In the NIEs, governments are tending to play a less paternalistic role than in the early 1980s, with moves towards a more relaxed wage policy in Singapore and a growth of union power in Korea. In South East Asia, in spite of minimum wage and lay-off regulations still on the books, labour markets are increasingly flexible. In Malaysia, where only one-sixth of the wage employees are unionised (and more than half of those are in the public sector), the Malaysian Trade Union Congress has been weakened by the recognition of other labour confederations, in-house unions have been encouraged, and casualisation of employment has increased (Jomo, 1991). In the Philippines flexibility is a 'growing reality' (Ofreneo, 1991:32), with job subcontrating, agency hiring, casualisation and special incentives to small, rural, low-wage manufacturing enterprises. In Indonesia the labour market, though ostensibly regulated, looks flexible and relatively unsegmented (Godfrey, 1991: 67–73).

South Asia, in contrast, still has a reputation for rigidity. In India, Mukhopadhay (1989:11) describes the 'dependent and avaricious mentality' of the big trade unions, which have acquired 'rights without responsibilities' and made the large firms into 'high wage islands'. Employment security is such that, 'in South Asia, it is almost impossible for an enterprise to reduce its work force except through liquidation, or by natural attribution through retirement. Employers will have to find new jobs for the workers they have hired, even if markets shrink or technology changes make part of the work force redundant. Labour is virtually a fixed cost of the enterprise' (ILO–ARTEP, 1987:53). This accurately describes the situation in some parts of the organised sector. What is less clear is the extent of its overall impact. India's successful achievement of substantial real effective devaluation (discussed in the previous section) in recent years suggests that its labour market may be less rigid than it looks. Labour market reform has been on the political agenda in China since the late 1970s, but it is fair to say that implementation has not been particularly fast. By mid-1991 86 per cent of state employees were still on lifetime contracts, such enterprises still have huge numbers of surplus workers, and the pay system is still unreformed (*China Daily*, 29 and 30 July 1991).

Reforms of *financial systems* have been attempted in many countries of the region, usually covering the development of banks, non-bank financial institutions, and the capital market; liberalisation of the external capital account; reduction of intermediation costs; and stronger regulation and supervision. Of the NIEs Hong Kong and Singapore have the most advanced financial sectors, and both have consolidated their position in the past two years. In South East Asia, Thailand introduced financial reforms in 1990, Malaysia deregulated further in 1991, and in the Philippines reforms introduced since 1986 have strengthened the banking sector but have been impeded by the foreign exchange crisis. In Indonesia the current emphasis is on stronger supervision, after deregulation set off a spectacular expansion in the number of banks and financial institutions and in the level of activity in the capital market. South Asia is lagging in this area of reform also. India's state banking sector makes low profits, there are many controls, and government budget deficits and the foreign exchange crisis have limited the pace of reform; and controls and regulations remain substantial in Bangladesh and Pakistan, in spite of recent attempts at reform.

A common element in the successful examples of outward-looking, labour-intensive development, finally, has been fiscal reform. Virtually all countries in the region have introduced tax reforms, simplifying and strengthening direct and indirect tax systems, to the benefit of yields. The NIEs and most South East Asian countries have also managed to restrain government expenditure (including privatisation in some cases, most notably that of Malaysia), and so significantly improve their fiscal position. Sometimes deficit-eliminating zeal may go too far. In Indonesia, for instance, there is a rigorous balanced budget convention but, since balance is defined as between total expenditure (including external debt service) and total revenue (including aid and revenue raised from oil companies), this has had a pro-cyclical effect: when oil revenues rise, government expenditure rises in parallel; when they fall, government spending has to be cut—arguably to the detriment of employment in recent years. South Asian governments have been slower to gain control of their budgets, although Sri Lanka and Pakistan have introduced important reforms, and, most recently, India has substantially reduced its deficit in the 1991–92 budget, which included a cut in fertiliser subsidies, removal of the sugar subsidy and an increase in prices of petroleum products.

In general, the pace of institutional reform has been much slower than that of price reform. This is not surprising. Institutional reform is more difficult. But it does suggest a possible answer to the question asked at the end of the previous section: was all that pain really necessary? The answer is, probably not. Maybe there is a trade-off between price reform and institutional reform: the larger the extent and the faster the pace of institutional reform, the smaller the price reforms that are needed to get an economy moving along these new paths. If institutional reform is hesitant, huge devaluations and falls in real wages may be needed to entice investors and employers out of their shells. In extreme cases, in the absence of institutional reform, no factor price changes will be large enough to tempt them into action.

1.5.3   Safety Nets

The pain of the new model can be minimised, also, by various short-run measures, which, in a labour-surplus economy, need not jeopardise the long-term objectives of the strategy. Such measures, sometimes described as safety nets, have the general effect of increasing the demand for labour. Apart from anything else, they may be essential for securing political support for the new, harsh strategy.

In China, for instance, an important role is played by the labour service companies. In addition to acting as employment exchanges and training agencies, these companies operate as safety nets, offering employment in productive enterprises to job-seekers. Thus, a state enterprise with surplus workers, instead of making them redundant, might set them up in business, running a restaurant or a shop. Over 200,000 of these companies have been created, with 17,500 million yuan in fixed assets, 14,800 million yuan in working capital and an annual income of 90,700 million yuan. In mid-1991 they employed 8.2 million workers (Pan Feng and Li Xi-Zheng, 1991). They may offend the principles of pure market forces, but in an economy undergoing traumatic structural change, particularly one with vast, profitable investment opportunities in the underdeveloped trade and services sectors, they may be an essential means of achieving labour market efficiency without social instability.

In other types of economy, with fewer easily identifiable investment opportunities for surplus workers, alternative types of safety net may be more appropriate. One of the most promising is the scheme of guaranteed employment at a minimum income for all persons willing to work. Such schemes have operated in rural India for some years, but as yet only on a relatively small scale. Bangladesh and Indonesia have also had some success with labour-intensive public works programmes. In principle such programmes create employment *directly* during the construction process, *indirectly* through linkages to supplying industries, *through the multiplier* when workers spend their earnings, and *dynamically* when the assets that have been built (schools, roads, health centres, etc.) help to raise productivity and income in the area and when the increase in demand raises the incentive to invest.

The best known employment guarantee scheme, in operation since the early 1970s and, since 1989, the model for a national programme, is that of Maharashtra state in western India. Persons aged eighteen or more are guaranteed unskilled work, at the minimum wage or above and at a reasonable distance from their homes, on the creation of productive assets for agriculture. A recent study of the Maharashtra scheme, carried out for ILO-ARTEP (Acharya, 1990), drew the following lessons from it.

(*i*) The employment offered needs to be for a relatively long period say, three to four months. (*ii*) The spatial distribution of projects has to be such as to minimise migration. Schemes should be matched to locations and to the timing and nature of the required work. (*iii*) Schemes should form part of the total development plan of an area, with emphasis on their impact on output. (*iv*) Wages should be reasonably high, to alleviate poverty and stabilise agricultural wages in the region. (*v*) Inter-departmental communication (absent in Maharashtra) is needed for a successful balancing of the roles of such schemes. (*vi*) A scientific and just formula is needed for distribution of funds between regions.

The only one of these conclusions that looks potentially dangerous is that concerning wage levels. As Sen (1975: 135) has pointed out, if programme wage rates exceed market wage rates, the numbers wanting to work on public works programmes tend to exceed the numbers that can be hired. This means that employment may have to be 'rationed' by project managers, increasing the temptation of corruption and making it more likely that those who work on the project will not consist only of those in the most desperate circumstances. An alternative system, explored by

Sen, would be to decentralise decisions about wage levels to project managers, moving them into line with local conditions.

The overall verdict on the Maharashtra scheme is mixed. It has "provided over 2,000 million person days of work to millions of workers since the mid-seventies. This has certainly provided the much needed respite to workers at times when they have needed work. Poverty has reduced. and the workers' levels of living have risen. Evaluation studies have however shown that the EGS has been found wanting on many counts. Nevertheless, it provides rich experience to others who plan to initiate such a scheme" (Acharya, 1990:58). Moreover, it should be emphasised that, while the short-term employment benefits to be gained from the construction process in projects of this kind are usually stressed, the return on the assets created by the projects (if carefully chosen) will continue for many years to come. They are not just short-term 'make-work' programmes but can make a vital long-term contribution to raising productivity, income and employment.

1.5.4   *Human Resource Development*

In the longer run a successful transition from labour surplus to labour shortage may well depend, in part, on the quality of an economy's human resources. In particular, as wages rise in a tightening labour market, the speed and ease of restructuring towards higher-technology, higher-skill and higher-value-added products may rest on the availability of educated and adaptable workers. Thus an activist human resource development policy, going beyond what would result from market forces

It has to be admitted that firm empirical evidence in support of this proposition is difficult to find. A recent review of issues and evidence in the field, published by ILO-ARTEP (Behrman, 1990), found several a priori reasons in support of an activist policy, including the possibility of important informational externalities in exploring new factor and product markets, increasing returns to scale, and significant public-goods aspects of knowledge. However, "while there is some evidence that human resources contribute to development in general and to growth in particular, there is virtually no evidence that the social gains exceed the private gains so that pro-human resource policies are warranted beyond the ones associated with basic education and health" (Behrman, 1990:90). The furthest that the author is willing to go is to recognise that the empirical studies presented to date may, in the view of some, "satisfy the criteria for a civil case of creating a presumption 'more likely than not' in favour of the case."

Clearly more research is needed on these issues. Behrman 1990:90 emphasises the need to try to distinguish between causality and association by controlling for other factors and taking care about the direction of causality, and suggests externalities and interactions between human resource investments and comparative advantage in particular sectors as areas for research. He concludes that "such research requires good data, care in estimation and interpretation, and sensitivity to specific details of particular cases, but the payoff might be considerable."

Meanwhile, governments cannot wait for research results and have to proceed on the basis that an activist human resource development policy will 'more likely than not' help to increase productivity, the incentive to invest in new sectors, and the demand for labour. As Table 11 shows, achievements so far in this respect vary widely between countries.

The best general indicator is probably the UNDP's index of educational attainment (in the final column of the table) which combines the influence of the adult literacy rate and mean years of schooling. As can be seen, several Asian developing economies are already exceeding or approaching the scores of the NIEs on this index, including Thailand, Western Samoa, the Philippines, Sri Lanka and Vietnam. Interestingly, apart from Thailand, this is not a list of the region's most dynamic economies. What it perhaps suggests is the enormous *potential* of economies like the Philippines, Sri Lanka and Vietnam, once their processes of institutional, political, administrative and social, as well as price, reforms have got under way. At the other extreme, the low scores of some of the South Asian economies (Nepal, Pakistan, Bangladesh and India) point to a need for huge investments in human resources.

The only indicator of quality in the Table, the primary pupil/teacher ratio, has its ambiguities; the ratio is higher than average in the Republic of Korea, for instance. But the countries with the lowest educational attainment (Bangladesh, India, Pakistan) also have the highest primary pupil/teacher ratios. This is particularly worrying in the light of international evidence that the return to improving quality is higher than to merely expanding quantity at the same average quality (e.g., see Behrman and Birdsall, 1983). Improvement in the quality of basic education, particularly in literacy and mathematics, increases the flexibility of the labour force and lays the basis for lifelong human resource development. Quality of education (and the capacity to innovate and adapt) may be more important for the introduction of new technologies and new types of skill than the prior existence of particular occupational categories.

In terms of future comparative advantage, also, the secondary enrolment ratio may be one of the most important indicators. Here there are some interesting anomalies. On the whole, the list of over-achievers is similar to that for the educational attainment index (Sri Lanka, several Pacific islands, Malaysia, Indonesia, China, Vietnam). But look at Thailand and India. Thailand has the lowest secondary enrolment ratio in South East Asia, apart from Lao PDR. And India does much better than would have been expected from its scores on other indices. Thai planners are aware of the problem posed by the low enrolment rate, and the new five year plan (1991–96) is to give priority to increasing the transition rate from primary to secondary school. But the impact of such an increase is long delayed. Sussangkarn (1991:16) has calculated that, even if the transition rate from primary to secondary school were raised to 100 per cent by 1992, the proportion of workers with primary schooling and below would still be 72 per cent in the year 2000. So substantial increases in non-formal education and training are needed for workers who are already in the labour force. In India, on the other hand, although agricultural development may be constrained by low literacy rates, growth in other leading sectors may be sustained by the relatively high rates of secondary enrolment and output.

Official statistics can usefully be supplemented by the views of businessmen. Table 12 shows the results of a survey conducted by the Hong Kong based Political Economic Risk Consultancy Ltd, reported in the *International Herald Tribune* of 29, July 1991.

As can be seen, the countries in the Table (Japan, the NIEs and South East Asian Economies) fall into three categories, as far as production labour is con-

TABLE 11

Human Resource Development Indicators in Selected Asian Economies

	Enrolment Ratios			Primary pupil/teacher ratio 1986–88	Adult literacy rate 1985	Mean years of schooling 1980	Index of educational attainment
	Primary	Secondary	Tertiary				
Newly Industrialising Economies							
Hong Kong	—	74	—	27	88	6	61
Korea, Rep.	100	86	38	36	95	7	65
Singapore	100	69	—	26	83	4	57
South East Asia							
Indonesia	100	48	—	24	72	3	49
Lao PDR	—	27	2	27	50	3	34
Malaysia	—	57	7	21	74	4	51
Philippines	98	71	28	33	88	7	61
Thailand	—	28	—	19	91	4	62
Vietnam, Soc. Rep.	88	42	—	—	84	3	57
South Asia							
Bangladesh	63	17	5	60	32	2	22
India	—	41	6	46	44	2	30
Myanmar	—	24	5	43	78	3	53
Nepal	—	30	5	37	22	2	16
Pakistan	—	19	5	41	31	2	21
Sri Lanka	100	71	4	32	87	6	60
China, People's Rep.	100	44	2	23	68	5	47

(Contd.)

TABLE 11 (*Contd.*)

Human Resource Development Indicators in Selected Asian Economies

	Enrolment Ratios			Primary pupil/teacher ratio 1986–88	Adult literacy rate 1985	Mean years of schooling 1980	Index of educational attainment
	Primary	*Secondary*	*Tertiary*				
Pacific Islands							
Fiji	100	56	—	30	80	5	55
Papua New Guinea	73	13	2	32	47	1	31
Solomon Islands	—	19	—	21	45	1	30
Vanuatu	—	57	—	24	53	4	37
Western Samoa	—	70	—	27	90	5	62
Asian Developing Countries	—	46	7	25	72	5	50
All Developing Countries	90	41	34	35	60	4	41
All Developed Countries	90	—	—	19	—	9	—

Notes: — not available,

Index of educational attainment = 2/3 x adult literacy rate + 1/3 x mean years of schooling.

Source: *Human Development Report, 1991.* UNDP, OUP, New York.

cerned: labour-surplus economies with the lowest possible cost and highest availability (China, Indonesia, Vietnam); an intermediate category with slight cost or availability problems (Malaysia, the Philippines, Thailand); and labour-shortage economies (Japan, Hong Kong, Singapore, Republic of Korea and Taiwan–China). The variations in views on the quality of labour are largely in line with what would be expected from Table 11. Japan and the NIEs get the best score, while Malaysia, the Philippines and Vietnam are rated slightly ahead of Thailand, Indonesia and China. The challenge of human resource development facing South East Asia's labour-abundant economies is highlighted by the poor ratings given to the quality of managerial labour in China, Indonesia, Thailand and Vietnam; in this respect also Malaysia and the Philippines are in an intermediate position.

TABLE 12

Labour Ratings in Selected Asian Countries

	Production Labour			Managerial Labour		
	Q	A	C	Q	A	C
China	5	1	1	10	10	1
Hong Kong	1	10	8	1	10	10
Indonesia	5	1	1	10	10	2
Japan	1	10	10	1	1	10
Malaysia	3	3	3	5	5	5
Philippines	3	1	2	3	1	1
Singapore	1	10	8	1	10	8
Korea, Republic	1	8	7	5	10	9
Taiwan-China	1	9	8	1	8	9
Thailand	4	2	1	10	10	4
Vietnam	3	1	1	10	5	1

Notes: Q= Quality; A = Availability; C = Cost
1 = the best grade possible; 10 = the worst grade

Source: Political and Economic Risk Consultancy Ltd, reported in *International Herald Tribune*, 29, July 1991.

1.5.5 Sequencing of Policy

There is an obvious sequence of policies for transition from labour surplus to labour shortage. Policies to take up whatever slack may exist in the labour market, through measures to increase the demand for labour such as guaranteed employment schemes, operate in the *short term*. They help to monitor the state of the labour market, and, if properly designed, automatically fade away as the need for them subsides. This would happen in the *medium term* if reform of institutions and factor prices is successful. And in the *longer term* it is to be hoped that the beneficial impact of an activist human resource development policy would begin to be felt.

1.6 Prospects

To prevent an already long review from becoming even longer, it may be useful to summarise in a Table, on the basis of our discussion so far, the prospects for further progress along the road towards labour shortage of the region's main economies.

Much, of course, depends, in such increasingly outward-looking economies, on the prospects for the world economy and for international trade. In this respect the assumptions underlying Table 13 are similar to those of the World Bank's 'baseline scenario' (World Bank, 1991:27), i.e. moderately favourable external conditions.[1]

TABLE 13

Prospects for Economies and Labour Markets in Developing Asia

	Economy	*Labour Market*
Hong Kong	Re-export growth will pick up again. Port and air-port development strategy under way. Inflation still high.	Continued shortage of skilled and unskilled labour. Wage increases particularly in construction, finance, trade. Pressure for more labour imports.
Korea, Rep.	Government measures will slow construction growth, but export-led growth in real GDP will accelerate, as markets recover.	Acute labour shortage will hamper government efforts to keep wage increases to single figures. Maybe fewer strikes and lock-outs.
Singapore	Fast output and export growth, based on more diverse manufacturing sector and export markets, and flourishing services.	Danger that unit labour costs may begin to rise as shortage gets more acute. Confusion on labour import policy needs to be cleared up.
Taiwan–China	Government spending on projects main thrust behind gradual acceleration in GDP growth, but exports also buoyant.	Labour shortages will in-crease upward pressure on wages and encourage use of foreign labour. Retraining needed for high-tech industries.
Malaysia	Amid fears of overheating, rising prices and current account deficit, growth may slow slightly, but is still likely to exceed 7% p.a.	Continued shortage of skilled and unskilled labour will lead to increased training, and import of foreign workers.

(Contd.)

---

1.   In more detail, the baseline scenario assumes: a gently upward trend in the real price of oil; a reduction in the US structural fiscal deficit; mild and short-lived recession in the US and some other industrialised countries; policy reforms leading to faster growth in productivity in Europe and Japan; continued high real interest rates in the medium term; substantial progress in Uruguay Round negotiations except for agriculture; significant growth benefits for Europe from the 1992 measures; a gradual increase in net inflows of capital into developing countries, most of which will continue to implement policy reforms.

TABLE 13 (*Contd.*)

Prospects for Economies and Labour Markets in Developing Asia

	Economy	Labour Market
Thailand	Growth will be only slightly slower than in recent years, still over 7% p.a. But tight monetary and fiscal policies will ease inflationary pressures.	Despite attempts to control public-sector wages, structural change in labour market will mean continued key shortages.
Indonesia	Export and tourism earnings up, but tight budget policy will moderate growth in consumption and investment. GDP growth still healthy and inflation rate low.	Continued increase in demand for labour, but not yet at turning point. Educated unemployment still a problem.
Philippines	Tight budgetary policy and sluggish export demand will mean even slower growth in 1991. Some improvement then expected, but not maintainable in absence of structural reforms.	Falling industrial and stagnant agricultural employment only offset by rise in residual services employment. Cyclical improvement from 1992, but structural dependence on overseas employment continues.
Vietnam	Given continued commitment to reform and availability of inputs, agriculture will revive and industrial growth accelerate. Longer-term prospects depend also on normalisation of relations with US.	Demand for labour will increase, particularly in industry. But demobilisation return of migrants and labour force growth will ensure continued labour surplus.
India	The 1991–92 budget and new industrial policy mark a change in direction, favourable to growth, particularly in industry. Given political stability, revival may come by 1992.	Immediate employment prospects difficult. Medium-term recovery and normalisation in Gulf will boost demand for labour, but still excess supply.
Pakistan	If momentum of recent de-regulation and privatisation measures is maintained, industrial boom may result. Continued agricultural growth also likely.	Impact of faster growth on demand for labour may be relatively small, to judge from past experience. Labour market may continue to be slack.

(Contd.)

TABLE 13 (*Contd.*)

Prospects for Economies and Labour Markets in Developing Asia

	Economy	Labour Market
Bangladesh	Despite natural disasters, industry and services are expected to revive, due to increased public investment, incentives for private sector and export demand. But effects of cyclone will be felt for long time.	Still a chronically labour-surplus economy. Real wages in agriculture and industry unlikely to rise.
Sri Lanka	One of South Asia's most hopeful cases. Provided political and climatic factors are favourable, boom in industry and tourism should continue, backed by solid agricultural growth.	Growth in private sector and return to normal in Gulf will boost demand for labour. Partly offset by civil service cuts. Educated labour force will be great asset as economy changes.
Papua New Guinea	New mining, oil and gas developments promise resumed growth, but only if law and order problem is solved.	Economic revival should increase demand for labour in private sector, but offset by public sector cuts.
Fiji	Fall in growth rate looks likely, as sugar, tourism and garments all run into problems. Longer-term prospects depend on market diversification.	Shortages of skilled labour will persist, but demand for unskilled labour may grow more slowly. Labour market increasingly de-regulated and trade unions weakened.
China	Government has continued difficulty in controlling growth process. Faster growth, but with inflationary dangers.	Slow progress in reform. Rigidity means wages grow faster than productivity in state enterprises.

Sources: Asian Development Bank (1991); The Economist Intelligence Unit, *Country Reports* on the above countries, No.2, 1991; World Bank (1991).

In short, as can be seen from Table 12, the expectation is of an intensification of labour shortage in the NIEs, with increasing pressure for imports of labour. In South East Asia, Malaysia will also be relying increasingly on foreign workers; in Thailand and Indonesia, although the demand for unskilled workers will be increasing fast, shortages, as yet, will only occur in the case of skilled and professional/managerial workers; Vietnam is only at the beginning of a painful but promising process of reform; and the Philippines is likely to continue to lag behind the others in this area. In South Asia, India, Pakistan and Bangladesh are moving in the right direction but the trends are most promising in Sri Lanka, which may at last begin to enjoy a return on its heavy investment in education. And the absence of effective labour market reform in China will limit the gains to labour from economic growth.

Almost all the region's developing economies, at different points on the road to labour shortage, are pursuing the new, outward-looking model of getting prices right and removing institutional obstacles to the better working of markets. In general, they have moved faster to reform prices than to reform institutions. This has been extremely painful, involving huge devaluations and falls in real wages. It is probable that, if institutional reform had been faster, the price reforms needed to get these economies moving along new paths would have been smaller, and the whole process less painful. More use, also, could probably be made of safety net measures, such as guaranteed employment schemes, designed to reduce the pain of the new harsh strategy without, in a labour-surplus economy, jeopardising its long-term objectives. Meanwhile the basis can be laid for a successful transition, in the longer run, from labour surplus to labour shortage, by an activist human resource development strategy.

Finally, in tracking progress along this road, we have hoped to show how much more revealing of labour market situations and of changes over time is analysis of real wages, wage employment and value added per worker than is analysis of labour force surveys. This suggests a new and exciting agenda for Asia's employment planners—the development of alternative indicators that will be of urgent interest to policy-makers, instead of surveys that are ignored by all except academics.

References

Acharya, Sarthi, 1990. 'The Maharashtra Employment Guarantee Scheme: A Study of Labour Market Intervention', ILO-ARTEP Working Paper, New Delhi, May.

Asian Development Bank, 1991. *Asian Development Outlook 1991*, Manila.

Behrman, Jere R., 1990. *Human Resource Led Development? Review of Issues and Evidence*, ILO-ARTEP, New Delhi.

Behrman, Jere R. and Nancy Birdsall, 1983. 'The Quality of Schooling: Quantity Alone Is Misleading', *American Economic Review*, 73, 928-46.

Godfrey, Martin, 1991. 'Surplus Labour Re-specified: Theory, Measurement and Policy for Indonesia', Report to the Economic and Social Committee for Overseas Research, IDS, Sussex University, June.

ILO-ARTEP, 1990a. The Gulf Crisis and the Sri Lanka Economy: The Impact and Implications (mimeo.), New Delhi, October.

ILO-ARTEP, 1990b. The Economic Impact of the Gulf Crisis on the Indian Economy, with Special Reference to Kerala and Measures for Re-absorption of Return Migrants (mimeo.), New Delhi, December.

ILO-ARTEP, 1991a. The Economic Impact of the Gulf Crisis in Pakistan and Measures for Productive Reabsorption of Return Migrants (mimeo.), New Delhi, February.

ILO-ARTEP, 1991b. The Economic Imˀˀact of the Gulf Crisis on the Bangladesh Economy (mimeo.), New Delhi, February.

Jomo, K.S., 1991. 'Malaysian Labour Market Adjustments in a Period of Structural Change', Paper presented at ILO-ARTEP Regional Technical Workshop on Labour Market Analysis as a Tool for HRD Planning, Beijing, July.

Kemal, A.R., 1990. 'Protection, Industrial Development and Employment Generation in Pakistan', The Asian HRD Planning Network, Working Paper, ILO-ARTEP, New Delhi.

Lewis, W.A., 1954 'Economic Development with Unlimited Supplies of Labour', Manchester School of Economic and Social Studies, 22.2.

Mahmood, Moazam, 1991. 'The Implications of Rural Labour Market Analysis for Generating Rural Employment in South Asia', Asian Network of HRD Planning Institutes, ILO-ARTEP, New Delhi, April.

Mohanty, Mritiunjoy, 1991. Labour Demand and Migration in Japan and Hong Kong (mimeo.), ILO-ARTEP, New Delhi.

Ofreneo, Rene E., 1991. 'Labour Market Adjustments in the Philippines in a Period of Structural Changes', Paper presented at ILO-ARTEP Regional Technical Workshop on Labour Market Analysis as a Tool for HRD Planning, Beijing, July.

Pan Feng and Li Xi-Zheng, 1991. 'For a System of Administration of the Labour Force and an Operating Mechanism Integrating a Planned Economy with Market Regulation', Paper presented at ILO-ARTEP Regional Technical Workshop on Labour Market Analysis as a Tool for HRD Planning, Beijing, July.

Planning Commission, Government of India, 1990. 'Employment: Past Trends and Prospects', Working Paper, New Delhi, May.

Ranis, Gustav and J.C.H. Fei, 1961. 'A Theory of Economic Development', *American Economic Review*, 51.4, 533-65.

Sen, A.K., 1975. *Employment, Technology and Development*, OUP, London.

Sussangkarn, Chalongphob, 1991. 'Thai Economic Growth, Emerging Labour Market Problems and Policy Responses', Paper presented at ILO-ARTEP Regional Technical Workshop on Labour Market Analysis as a Tool for HRD Planning, Beijing, July.

US Department of Labour, 1991. 'Labour Shortages in East Asian Countries', *Foreign Labour Trends*, 3, Washington.

Discussion

The principal discussant Mr Yau de Piyau of the Ministry of Human Resources, Malaysia began his review saying that it is debatable whether aiming at labour shortages, the ultimate message of Dr Martin Godfrey's paper, is practical and feasible with regard to all Asian countries. The proposed strategy may be of use in the NIEs, but in countries with large populations and labour forces, it is doubtful if it can be followed.

Even for the NIEs, there are number of factors that have not been taken into account in the paper and that may impede the success of strategies advocated, such as: (a) the flow of capital from Asia to Eastern Europe and South America; (b) the emergence of regional blocs, such as the EC, and the threat of protectionism which would imply a loss of markets for nations aiming at export growth; (c) the practice of tying up aid with human and democratic rights; and (d) the question whether the industrialised countries will allow the developing world to 'catch up' with them.

Mr Yau then questioned Dr Godfrey's proposition that wages can be used as instruments of measurement, since they are to aggregative to really be of any value to employment planners. He questioned whether figures on the self-employed should be left out and called for discussion on this point. He also observed that the five policy measures presented in the paper have been implemented in a few countries with positive results. (In Malaysia, a tripartite consensus has been achieved on linking wages to productivity and workers' contributions.)

In relation to human resource development, Mr Yau said that he would have liked Dr Godfrey to touch upon vocational skills training, retraining and skills upgrading, which is becoming increasingly important as new technologies are introduced and higher productivity is strived for. Giving an example from Malaysia, Mr Yau explained that labour shortages are being experienced by workers at the semi-skilled level, at production-lines and on shop floors. The Malaysian government is trying to remedy this by giving incentives to entrepreneurs during a 5-year period to shift to less labour-intensive production methods. To follow up the policy, labour market studies will be carried out every year during the period.

Contributing to the general discussion of the paper, a Malaysian participant claimed that rather than being an alternative, the analysis of wage statistics should complement existing methods. It also necessary to take into account the varying levels of development in different Asian countries which would make wage rate indicators more applicable in some of them than in others. According to the Malaysian experience, once labour shortages have been achieved, one is faced with a new set of problems since economic growth is impeded. One way of getting around this is to improve the labour force participation rate of women, especially in countries where it is low.

The employers' representative from Pakistan noted how, despite the absence of proper data, for many years, papers and material based on these data have been presented, discussed and implemented, although the assumptions in them are not realistic. The question must be asked, how can planners plan at all, without data? It necessarily follows that planning is based on inadequate data. The basic requirement for any planner is good quality data.

A participant from the Phillippines questioned the distinction between price reform and institutional reform in Dr Godfrey's paper, indicating that based on two examples from the Phillippine experience, institutional reform is usually undertaken precisely as a means to bring about price reform.

A Nepalese participant commented that problems would always be associated with the use of any indicator, especially since it is often difficult to obtain reliable data. It would be necessary to choose a set of indicators that would complement each other and that would be reasonable in terms of reliability and availability. The components of this set would have to vary from country to country. The participant also voiced the opinion that the policy issues listed by Dr Martin Godfrey would perhaps be of secondary importance in a nation's overall policies. They would have to be incorporated in overall development and macro-economic policies.

A Bangladesh participant felt that the paper was addressed more to NIEs even though a category of 'other countries' is mentioned in it. The labour force of Bangladesh is as large as that of all NIEs together, which makes Dr Godfrey's strategies difficult to apply there.

A workers' representative from India suggested that the private sector should take more responsibility for training. This would better satisfy the needs of specific industries as well as help ease shortages of certain types of skilled labour. Problems prevalent in India, particularly in the rural sector, are high unemployment rates alongside high wage rates due to collective bargaining in sectors such as coal mining.

A participant from Bhutan voiced the opinion that Dr Godfrey's suggestions would not be feasible in a country like Bhutan, a landlocked, mountainous LDC without financial resources. He also called for more dialogue between the North and the South on labour-related issues.

An Indonesian participant wondered whether it would not be possible, in economies where labour shortages and labour surpluses occur simultaneously, to train workers belonging to the surplus group in skills so that they could fill the labour shortage gaps.

Responding to Mr Yau's points, Dr Martin Godfrey said that the same kind of pessimistic views about the global context were prevalent fifteen years ago, and no one would have anticipated the emergence of the NIEs. Thus, one should not attach too much importance to such factors, nations will continue to develop despite them. He agreed that disaggregation of wages by sector, occupation, sex, etc. is indeed necessary.

He agreed with the representatives from Bhutan and Bangladesh that a labour shortage strategy is not very relevant for these countries. He also agreed that the use of wage rates as indicators could very well serve as a complement to other methods and that they should be viewed together with the institutional context in each country. A wage increase need not always be a sign of labour shortage. Dr Godfrey explained that he had not accounted for technical training in his paper since he considers this largely to be the responsibility of enterprises. An environment conducive to this should, however, be created to encourage enterprises to take on training. Finally, in reply to the query from an Indonesian participant, he said that the problem of labour shortages occurring at the same time as surpluses must have its origins either in the educational system not functioning as it should or in the educated labour not adjusting to the market situation.

2

Labour Market Analysis and Human Resource Development Planning[1]

M. MUQTADA

2.1 Introduction

Human resource development (HRD) planning has received increased attention in recent years from policy planners, practitioners, academics and international agencies.[2] There have also been initiatives in examining the possibilities and framework of an integrated approach to HRD planning, i.e. linking the development planning of a country with the major human resource variables. Furthermore, HRD planning has been posited in the form of a paradigm where protagonists contend that countries could possibly change their comparative advantages from primary commodity and low skill-intensive products to greater skill-intensive goods through deliberate expansion of human resources.[3]

While, on the one hand, HRD planning is, for a variety of reasons, being underscored, on the other hand, there have occurred, in the recent period, various reforms and structural changes in the Asian economies which implicitly tend to delimit the scope of HRD planning. The proponents of this view not only doubt the validity of HRD-led growth,[4] but also the basic principles of whether there should be any central planning at all, let alone unbridled public planning of investments in education and training.[5] The concept and practice of manpower planning is challenged even more strongly. They argue that in the current context of a drive towards 'lesser government', the role of such planning should give way to labour market analysis. Can labour market analyses provide adequate guidelines to HRD planning and skills formation in an economy?

---

1. An earlier version of the paper was presented at ILO-ARTEP's Fourth Meeting of Asian Employment Planners, New Delhi, 17–19 December 1991.

2. In the Asia-Pacific region, ILO-ARTEP has conducted several research, advisory and training activities on HRD planning under its Asian HRD Network programme. Cf. Amjad (1987). The UNDP has undertaken several initiatives on 'human development', including an annual publication on the human dimensions of development. Cf. *Human Development Report, 1990*, UNDP.

3. See Krause (1989).

4. Cf. Behrman (1990).

5. Psacharopoulos (1991).

The scope of the present paper is to examine, in broad terms, the role of HRD planning in the context of economic development (section 2.2); the major theme and limitations of manpower planning as a central concept of HRD planning (section 2.3); the current structural adjustment reforms that have underscored the increasing importance of labour market analysis and some of its limitations (section 2.4); and the broad contours of labour market analysis as a tool for HRD planning (section 2.5). In section 2.6 we examine briefly the role of governments in HRD planning and the final section (2.7) provides a tentative conclusion.

2.2 Economic Development and HRD Planning

During the post-war period, when most countries of the Asian region attained independence, there was a clear commitment to universal literacy across all countries. Such investment was seen as serving to provide a basic need, almost like better diet and health. Apart from literacy and primary education levels, which still remain relatively low in many Asian economies, especially the South Asian economies, various forms of human capital were sought to be developed, since skills and knowledge were believed to be closely associated with economic growth.[1] The role of governments in human capital formation was predicated on several premises, such as: (*i*) there are several social benefits that accrue from increasing educational investments (e.g., externality and spill-over effects of such investment); (*ii*) support to human capital formation would lead to enhanced opportunities of employment and efficient utilisation of manpower; (*iii*) there are several factors due to which the private sector would shy away from financing schooling and training, etc., especially in economies with low levels of social infrastructure.

Human resource planning was thus undertaken from various standpoints, ranging from building up social infrastructure to growth and equity considerations. Irrespective of the rationale, there was considerable expansion of education and training institutions and investment across all developing countries. Needless to say, the outcomes have been quite different in the different countries with regard to the rates and levels of attainment in various educational categories (see Table 1). During the 1970s and 1980s, investment in human resources, more specifically public investment in the expansion of education and training, came to be viewed with caution and scepticism. This was a period which saw the emergence of the problems of skills-mismatches and the educated-unemployed. Apart from the general lack of demand for particular groups of the educated-unemployed (e.g., arts graduates), public sector employment, which absorbs tertiary graduates in large proportions, started slowing down considerably. While the pace of economic growth and macro-economic management dictated the generation and absorption of various skills, there was nonetheless a growing concern over the public role in education and skills development. This concern, which was particularly linked to the emerging labour markets in the individual countries, was not necessarily with human resource development planning *per se*, but with the relevance of the role of

---

1. See Schultz (1962) for an exposition of this relationship.

the public sector and the skills that were found to be out of tune with the changing needs. The public vocational and technical education system, in particular, confronted the challenge of coping with changing demand for relevant skills.

Human resource planning, despite the above scepticism, has during the 1980s, staged a come-back in various countries, albeit under varying rationale. In the case of Malaysia, human resource planning is seen to be crucial to resolve the human resource constraint to high-tech growth of the economy.[1] In the case of Thailand, human resource planning is seen as an important instrument to address the growing income disparities.[2] In Singapore, large dispersion of wages is associated with different educational categories, which calls for a rationalisation of its HRD planning.[3] Krause (1989) argues in favour of human resource policies for a variety of reasons, including the earnings outcome from increased productivity of the poor.

In the backdrop of the cyclical emphasis and de-emphasis of the role and significance of HRD planning there have emerged many and diverse viewpoints. The theme of HRD planning and economic growth has attracted a great deal of attention especially in the context of the recent experiences of industrialisation and modernisation in the NIEs. There is a current contention that many of the Asian countries (especially the ASEAN countries) are poised to shift their comparative advantage (from cheap labour-based exports to high-tech assimilation and production), through technological leap-frogging, or industrial catch-up. The bases for this contention are as follows. (*i*) These countries are well exposed to the new technologies and have developed the necessary skills and infrastructure. A few countries, e.g. Taiwan–China, have already started producing prototype (compatible) high-tech products that are similar to those patented by the multinational firms of the OECD countries. (*ii*) The new technologies are known to be knowledge-intensive rather than based on experience, which would allow them to circumvent the long-time element hitherto required in adopting earlier technologies. (*iii*) Skills, be they of scientists, engineers, system analysts or other semi-skilled people, are relatively much cheaper in these countries, and this would boost their international competitiveness. (*iv*) There are large markets in the third world countries which would induce growth of such technologies and possible risk capital for R&D expenditures in these countries.

Krause (1989), in this context, lends support to the contention, drawing examples from South Korea and Taiwan–China.[4] He argues:

> Human resource driven economies obtain their stimulus for growth from advances in technology. The process only requires receiving and assimilating technology that already exists. The process has been described as industrial catch-up. . . Hence education is a basic ingredient in industrial catch-up as the tool for creating an atmosphere where technology can be transplanted and adapted.

---

1. See Lucas and Verry (1989).
2. Sussangkarn (1991).
3. I. Islam (1989).
4. Also see Singer and Baster (1980).

TABLE 1

Educational Composition of the Labour Force, Asia

| | | Percentage of labour force with | | | | | |
| | No education | Primary schooling | | Secondary schooling | | Higher education | Mean Years of schooling |
		Incomplete	Complete	Incomplete	Complete		
Newly Industrialising Economies							
Hong Kong							
1981	7.6	17.6	19.1	21.3	26.2	8.1	8.8
Korea, Republic of							
1969	44.9	9.1	30.2	7.3	6.1	2.4	3.9
1980	14.8	1.1	33.2	18.5	23.4	9.1	8.0
Singapore							
1974	40.3	4.9	21.9	16.0	8.3	8.5	5.3
1980	21.9	3.0	46.4	18.4	6.3	4.0	6.0
Taipei, China							
1980	9.3	4.5	30.2	18.9	24.3	12.7	8.6
1983	8.9	5.1	32.7	17.7	24.0	11.5	8.4
China, People's Republic of							
1982	28.3	13.1	21.3	25.8	10.7	0.9	4.5
South East Asia							
Indonesia							
1978	31.6	23.1	35.7	5.3	3.8	0.5	3.9
1980	26.1	18.9	33.4	11.4	8.9	1.2	4.9
Malaysia							
1967	27.0	1.7	55.7	9.2	4.6	1.8	5.0
1980	17.9	17.1	23.4	22.9	16.1	2.6	6.5

(Contd.)

TABLE 1 (*Contd.*)

Educational Composition of the Labour Force, Asia

		Percentage of labour force with					
	No education	*Primary schooling*		*Secondary schooling*		*Higher education*	*Mean Years of schooling*
		Incomplete	*Complete*	*Incomplete*	*Complete*		
Philippines							
1980	7.8	21.3	27.4	15.1	12.7	15.7	7.0
Thailand							
1960	37.4	55.6	1.1	3.5	2.0	0.4	3.3
1980	10.1	64.2	7.0	11.2	4.1	3.4	4.6
South Asia							
Afghanistan							
1979	72.0	6.1	9.4	5.6	7.0	0.0	2.1
Bangladesh							
1981	62.4	15.9	4.1	10.7	5.5	1.5	2.4
India							
1961	89.9	5.2	2.1	1.9	0.3	0.6	0.5
1981	66.6	14.5	6.9	4.9	3.9	3.2	1.9
Pakistan							
1975	75.8	11.2	7.7	3.7	0.6	1.0	1.2
1981	65.9	7.4	5.2	16.4	2.4	2.7	2.5
Sri Lanka							
1963	22.2	27.9	41.9	2.7	3.2	2.1	5.3
1981	8.5	12.7	35.9	38.3	2.8	1.8	7.5

Source: George Psacharopoulos and A.M. Arriagada (1986), 561–74.

There are equally strong opposing views, not so much on promoting flexible human resource development as a general goal, but on trying to prepare a country's skills for technological leap-frogging and industrialisation. Deliberate expansion of education and training investment to attain a shift in comparative advantage has been seen as a misplaced concern. No causal relationship can be established, although some country examples may show some associational relationships.[1] A recent study by the IMF attempts to measure the contribution of the HRD factor in economic growth through a decomposition analysis.[2] Using data from 55 developing countries for 1970-85, the study shows the tangible impact of investment in human capital on economic growth (see Table 2). The study contends that "expenditures on improving human capital appear to have a substa... al effect on output growth when both public and private spending on the development of human resources (education, health care and on-the-job training) are taken into account."[3]

There is no firm and conclusive evidence on whether HRD planning and economic growth are causally related, but several studies show a strong associational relationship between the two. There is thus a prime facie case to pursue HRD planning in an economy. The recent contentions on HRD planning are related more to what constitutes a balanced and meaningful HRD strategy, and what role the public sector should play in the creation (supply) and utilisation (demand) of manpower. The following section reviews the nature of these debates.

2.3 Manpower Planning and Labour Market Analysis

An integral part of human resource development (HRD) planning is employment and manpower planning which seeks to identify and design policies and programmes to clear the market for labour in general, and for skilled/educated manpower in particular.[4] Human resource planning, therefore, not only involves an understanding of the extent and patterns of employment growth by various sectors of the economy, but also a broad assessment of the nature of jobs created by skills/educational categories in order to avoid 'critical shortages or surpluses' of trained manpower, and hence social costs.

One must recognise that the aggregate view of employment generation is only notional, since what would be required in reality is to assess the nature of jobs that exist, and the nature of jobs that can be created commensurate with the highly diverse backgrounds and aspirations of the job-seekers. In other words, a *thorough* labour market analysis must accompany a full employment generation programme, since segmentation and differentiation in labour markets, rural and urban, would imply a many-sided employment strategy that would focus, with varying policy weights, on the hierarchy of the entire job-creation spectrum.

A significant implication of this is to ask how the state can 'plan' employment vis-à-vis complex labour market issues. While the nature and character of economic

---

1. Behrman (1990).
2. Cf. Otani and Villanueva (1989).
3. ª Ibid.
4. Cf. Thamarajakshi (1988).

TABLE 2

Major Determinants of Growth in LDCs

	Growth rate of per capita real GNP	Portion contributed by[1]					
		Domestic savings rate[2]	Rate of investment in human capital[3]	Growth rate of exports[4]	Growth rate of population	Real interest rate on external debt[5]	Other factors[6]
All sample countries	2.7	2.3	0.7	2.6	-2.0	0.1	-1.0
High-income countries	4.0	3.7	0.3	3.5	-1.3	0.1	-2.3
Middle-income countries	2.0	7.5	2.3	0.6	-3.6	0.5	-5.3
Low-income countries	1.4	0.0	1.8	2.6	-3.1	0.4	-0.3

Notes: Low-income countries: average per capita nominal GNP of US $ 560 or below in 1970-85; middle-income countries: average per capita nominal GNP of more than US $ 560 but less than US $ 1,000; high-income countries: per capita nominal GNP of US $ 1,100 or above.
[1] Figures are expressed as annual averages
[2] Ratio of domestic saving to GNP
[3] Ratio of educational expenditure to GNP
[4] In real terms
[5] Nominal interest rate on external debt (denominated in US dollars) less the percentage change in export prices (in US dollars).

Source: Derived from Otani and Villanueva (1989).

growth may be planned and defined with greater employment weight, mere creation of job opportunities may not be able to realise a full employment situation. Low literacy rates, low levels of skills and diverse ethnicities, the low status of women, and the existence of scheduled castes and tribes in some countries, together imply that a substantial proportion of the labour force may not easily enter the labour market. The above categories represent vulnerable groups, who may be bypassed by the traditional process of economic growth and distribution. That is to say, for these vulnerable categories, special measures of job and income creation would have to be designed. But, while such special direct job creation schemes may be designed to reach these groups, one ought to be cautious that these, pervasive as they would be, do not create a continued programme-dependence, and do not degenerate into a peculiar labour market of their own, thereby segmenting the disadvantaged, unskilled workers from the mainstream job markets.

The above brings about the fact that aggregate employment planning would be a national macroeconomic exercise unless it embodies examination of labour market issues. Employment and manpower planning has, hitherto, been viewed as largely a derivative of output and investment planning in an economy. Historically, however, manpower planning in particular has been seen as an exercise to support economic *change*, through the development of human resources for efficient use. While that remained the broad *scope* of manpower planning, in practice, however, manpower planning appeared to be limited to a small percentage of the work force who were skilled or semi-skilled. This small proportion of the work force was seen as strategically significant, and dubbed as 'change agents' in the drive towards industrialisation and modernisation. During the 1950s and 1960s, there was thus a great emphasis on design and expansion of educational institutions ranging from formal schooling at primary, secondary and tertiary levels to various forms of training programmes. In retrospect, it appears that manpower planning pinned high hopes on the supply side of manpower development that would, in some undefined way, assist growth. In many countries, such hopes remained unfulfilled, and the 1970s and 1980s saw the emergence of large numbers of educated unemployed as a serious labour market concern. Apart from the long-gestation education programmes, even the vocational training system seemed to gradually become of marginal relevance to the needs of the changing situation. By and large, the non-formal systems of skills development and on-the-job training were not paid due attention.

Growth is a complex phenomenon, and human resource planning can perhaps contribute to sustaining growth in a number of ways. However, as shown by the case histories of Sri Lanka and the Philippines, which have attained a high degree of literacy and educational level, HRD planning is not a *sufficient* condition for growth to take place. In the case of the skilled labour force, supply need not generate its own demand. This is not to suggest that manpower planning has ignored demand-side considerations. Rather, demand-side issues have been rather narrowly incorporated, often through single mechanistic approaches.

It has been maintained that employment and manpower planning is a "process for ensuring efficiency of labour markets and is thus much wider than the mechanistic aspects of projections and forecasts."[1] In practice, however, manpower planning has come to be essentially associated with simple or complex (dis-aggregated) projects, considerably leaning towards what is known as the 'manpower requirements approach' (MRA), although other approaches, such as the 'rate of return approach' (RRA) and international comparison are also adopted. In point of fact, the manpower planning approach is often viewed synonymously with MRA. In its most simple form, MRA specifies the demand for labour, categorised in terms of skills or education, for various sectors, projected through a skills-flow table which is analogous to the inter-industry flow table (input-output method):

$$Hij = qij$$
$$\text{where, } Hij = i\text{th skill used in } j\text{th sector of production}$$
$$Xj = j\text{th sector's output}$$
$$qij = \text{'skill coefficient', assumed constant}$$

There are several variations that can be incorporated in such models, e.g. qij, which is assumed constant, can take on different values by introducing a range of alternative technologies. Such an approach to manpower planning has come under an array of criticism. As Hollister (1981) succinctly puts it, "authorities in the education and training sector must be made to understand that planners will not be able to tell them exactly how much and which types of manpower are required by a given date."[2]

Criticisms were first levelled against this approach on the empirical evidence that forecasts were inaccurate, and mostly off target[3] (see Table 3 on the South Korean experience). It must be pointed out that not all predictions based on MRA were necessarily wild.[4] However, apart from empirical contradictions, the MRA approach to manpower planning has been criticised on conceptual grounds as well. The more frequently forwarded limitation relates to the assumption that labour demand per unit of output remains unaffected by the scale of production. Therefore, it neither allows for an increase in productivity, nor for any substitution possibilities between skills.[5]

The manpower planning approach has been attacked from other standpoints as well: (*i*) the approach, in the context of many developing countries, is found to be inadequate in that it lacks an understanding of the nature of labour markets, the patterns of segmentation which may often be dictated by non-economic factors, such as ethnicity, in India.[6] This is of particular importance in countries which are attempting to work towards a full employment strategy, since the skills profile is often neglected in addressing a full employment concern.[7] (*ii*) Critics of

---

1. Ibid.
2. Cf. Hollister (1981).
3. See Debeauvais and Psacharopoulos (1985) for a detailed assessment and critique of the MRA approaches.
4. Cf. C. Colclough (1990), who argues that evidence is still inadequate 'for a rejection of manpower planning'.
5. Ibid.
6. Rodgers (1990).
7. See, for example, Planning Commission, India (1990).

planning are in general also critics of manpower planning. They argue that planning, which involves interventions, often introduces distortions in the efficient functioning of markets, including labour markets. The collapse of central planning in the USSR, Eastern Europe and elsewhere are cited as general examples,[1] and the logic is extended to manpower planning as well since it is linked to output/investment planning. (*iii*) The manpower planning approach also suffers from the lack of a data base that could provide more meaningful insights into labour market functioning. The rapidity of changes in skills requirements that actually take place cannot be precisely captured in such an approach.

Some of the above criticisms have been examined by Colclough (1990), who finds that not all of these are well-founded.[2] Nevertheless the manpower planning approach has been increasingly looked upon with scepticism, especially when seen as guiding development and diversification of education and training policies. As earlier pointed out, the manpower planning approach has been closely linked to the MRA approach. It should be emphasised that manpower planning, in practice, has also taken recourse to the rate of return approach, often to supplement the MRA approach, especially with regard to "investments in fields of education for the short and medium term where the projection approach is difficult to apply, as well as for long-term investments in skill formation where the gestation lag is long".[3] As is well-known, the rate of return approach also has inherent

TABLE 3

Prediction Errors of Projected Manpower Requirements by Sector and Occupation, Korea, 1980–85

Sector	Nature of Error
Primary	'Underprediction'
Secondary	'Overprediction'
Tertiary	'Overprediction' by KEDI, reverse by KDI
Occupation	
Professional & Technical	'Overprediction' by KEDI, reverse by KDI
Clerical	'Overprediction' by KEDI, reverse by KDI
Sales	'Underprediction' by KDI,
Sales	'Underprediction' by KDI, 'Insignificant Error' by KDI
Service	'Underprediction'
Farm	'Underprediction'
Production	'Overprediction'

Notes: KDI = Korea Development Institute
         KEDI = Korea Educational Development Institute

Source: Kim, Yoo Bee (1986). "Human Resource Planning: The Asian Experience—Republic of Korea", Paper presented at the Asian Network of Human Resource Development Planning Institutes Technical Workshop, Bangkok, 16-18 December, 1986.

1. Cf. Psacharopoulos (1991).
2. See Colclough (1990).
3. ILO-ARTEP (1984).

methodological and measurement difficulties, especially as regards imputation of social costs and benefits.

The discussion above does not necessarily imply that planning and forecasting would cease to play a role. In point of fact, the experience of the Asian countries, whether in planning for investment/output growth or employment generation, shows the use of and need for basic projections. Projecting basic labour supply-demand balances (Table 4), or projecting possible scenarios of restructuring of educational profiles (Table 5) are seen as not only providing useful insights, but also significant feedback to national and sectoral policy frameworks. These can act as a broad framework of base positions and desired objectives, within the projected social and economic goals of an individual country.

The opponents of the manpower planning approach would advocate such exercises to be treated within manpower analysis, other than be used as a precise guide to the educational and training outputs of the country. It is in the wake of the shortcomings of the manpower approach that the so-called 'new approach' of labour market analysis (also referred to as manpower analysis approach) is being advocated in the recent period. The labour market analysis approach (LMA), whose basic premise is that education and skills development should be based on signals from the

TABLE 4

**Growth Rate of Population, Labour Force Employment
and Unemployment Relative to GDP, Malaysia**

					(Per cent per annum)
	1961–70	1971–75	1976–80	1981–85	1985–89
GDP	5.3	7.3	8.5	5.7	6.5
Population	2.8	2.7	2.6	2.6	2.6
Labour force	3.1	3.6	3.5	3.9	3.7
Employment	2.8	4.6	3.7	3.4	3.8
Employment/GDP ratio (elasticity)	0.53	0.63	0.44	0.60	0.58

Sources: Wong (1983) for periods up to 1980; Fifth Malaysian Plan for 1980–85; various official data including annual Ministry of Finance and Bank Negara reports 1985–89. For years earlier than 1980 the growth rate of GDP relates to all Malaysia but the other statistics are for Peninsular Malaysia only.

TABLE 5

Projected Share of Work Force by Education, Thailand

	1991	1996	2000
Primary and Below	82.7	79.4	75.7
Lower Secondary	6.6	8.0	9.4
Upper Secondary	2.7	3.5	4.2
Tech. Vocational	1.3	1.7	2.2
University	3.9	4.3	4.7

Source: Sussangkarn (1991).

labour market, is rather general and has to be modified in the context of the issues and the country being examined. Such labour market signals could come from a variety of sources, viz. trends in wages and earnings, vacancy and labour turnover rates, establishment and tracer surveys, diagnostic studies of key labour market issues, key informants, etc. It must be pointed out that such an approach does not discount the merit of applying the rate of return approach in deciding investments in education and training. Labour market analysis simply contends that MRA is rather discontinuous, faulty and the forecasts are often wider off than even 'best guesses', whereas the labour market approach is more continuous and takes care of shorter-term details in the labour market functioning, including how on-the-job training can mitigate short-term skills imbalances in specific occupations and industries.

The context of the increasing emphasis on the labour market approach is discussed in the following section.

2.4   Flexibility and the Ascendancy of Labour Market Analysis

During the 1980s, most of the countries of Asia and the Pacific pursued an active structural adjustment programme, evidently to resolve their widening fiscal and current account deficits. This programme included, *inter alia*, various fiscal and financial reforms to mobilise and allocate resources more efficiently, trade liberalisation and rationalisation of public expenditure. The practical policy instruments required to implement such measures were deregulation (i.e. liberalisation of existing controls), and an *active* strategy of export promotion, privatisation and attraction of foreign capital. These necessarily entailed ajustments in the production system and restructuring.

Much before the structural adjustment advocacy of the 1980s many Asian countries, especially the NIEs, had already been experiencing fast firm-level restructuring. A well-defined export-oriented industrialisation programme was already in place, forestalled through various economic and institutional measures. During the 1980s, the structural adjustment programme, through its stance on anti-protection and liberalisation, underscored the urgency of industrial targeting and restructuring, to bring about greater efficiency and competition in the economy. Enterprise-level restructuring carried significant implications for labour market adjustment and employment. A trend observed over the recent past, especially during the last decade, is that labour market structure and conditions have been changing significantly.[1] It must be noted that these changes in the labour markets cannot be interpreted in isolation from the changes in the product and other factor markets which are directly affected in an adjustment process. It is also significant to note, in this context, the argument that the relatively better performance of the Asian economies has been facilitated by, among other factors, a well-functioning labour market.[2]

---

1. See Pang Eng Fong (ed.), *Labour Market Developments and Structural Change*, Singapore University Press, 1988. Also various articles in the special issue on 'High Tech and Labour in Asia' of *Labour and Society*, Vol. 14, 1989, International Institute of Labour Studies, ILO, Geneva.

2. P. Nolan, 'Assessing Economic Growth in the Asian NICs', *Journal of Contemporary Asia*, Vol. 20, No. 1, 1990.

In the search for factors explaining changing labour market conditions, it is necessary to look into country-specific experiences of structural changes that have occurred over the past two decades, and the individual country responses to adjustment. The NIEs and the ASEAN in particular, have followed a broad export-oriented industrialisation, with significant involvement of direct foreign investment, multinationals and export-processing zones. The recipient country has provided cheap labour as a complement to foreign resources and technology, mostly in the labour-intensive manufacturing export industries. The NIEs and Singapore, from among the ASEAN countries, have already lost their comparative advantage in labour-intensive exports, and rapid restructuring has taken place in order to cope with rising labour costs and labour shortages. Malaysia is already showing signs of tight labour markets, at least in such sectors as electronics. The Philippines, Indonesia and most other South Asian countries still retain large surpluses in labour, and in principle, a competitive edge in labour-intensive production, should foreign capital continue to be relocated in these countries.

The rapid structural changes in most Asian countries, including China, and the foreign ventures supporting the export-oriented industrialisation strategy have greatly influenced production systems, carrying implications for employment, wages, firm size, labour standards and industrial relations. How far structural adjustment measures enhance or adversely affect structural transformation and firm-level restructuring, and how far adjustment measures affect labour market conditions to enhance such transformation are complex issues and require intensive research.

There are, however, a few recent trends in labour markets that can be clearly observed. First, the labour markets are observed to be relatively more flexible, whether attained through interventions or perpetrated by the new technology transfer, joint ventures and the nature of outward-oriented industrialisation. The basic features of such flexibility are reflected in the rise of casualisation of labour, contract and piece-rated workers, subcontracting and linkages with micro-enterprises. ILO-ARTEP investigations in the Philippines and India (especially in the electronics sector) tend to support this.[1] Second, recent labour force statistics in some countries reveal a shift of the work force away from wage-employment to self-employment. This phenomenon was particularly registered during the mid-1980s in Malaysia, the Philippines and other countries where large-scale lay-offs took place in the organised sector and public sector employment.[2] Third, the skills composition of the work force has also been rapidly changing, as a response to changing demand for skills in various non-traditional production and exports industries. It must be noted that while the less developing countries with relatively less exposure to new technologies are trying to enhance 'computer literacy' to be able to absorb and utilise the new technologies, some of the more advanced developing countries have experienced the growth of high-skill pockets (for designing, software planning, component production, etc.) *as well as* lower-level skills (e.g., on-the-job training for assembly operations and export-oriented

---

1. Cf. Edgren (ed.), *Restructuring, Employment and Industrial Relations*, ILO-ARTEP, New Delhi, 1989.

2. The Malaysian example is treated comprehensively in R.E. Lucas and D. Verry (1989).

production processes). A study on HRD implications of ASEAN industrial restructuring shows that there are several instances of a 'deskilling' effect upon factory workers who are engaged in export-oriented production. On the other hand, countries facing labour shortages, e.g. Singapore, are encouraging multi-skilling programmes to cope with rapid enterprise restructuring and consequent displacements. Fourth, more and more women are participating in the labour markets, at various levels and in almost all occupations. While in the fast growing economies, the female work force has mitigated somewhat the growing labour shortages, in the slow growing economies, women have entered labour markets often to enhance and sustain the threshold income of the household. During the recession in the mid-1980s in the Philippines, women participated in the job market to supplement household incomes wnen real earnings of households started declining.[1] Given very limited job opportunities in the organised sector, it is needless to say that the bulk of such participation by women has been in informal sector activities.

With greater integration of domestic production to world economy, and in view of such adjustment measures as deregulation, trade liberalisation, privatisation and foreign exchange rate adjustments, there are clear compulsions for firms, export-oriented or otherwise, to adjust to these changes. Firms had to attain greater efficiency both in terms of pricing and quality to face domestic and external competition. Hence restructuring often entailed infusion of new technologies, reorganising the size and nature of operations, redefining factor proportions, retrenchments and increasing emphasis on on-the-job training and skills development. While structural adjustment has, in general, contributed to the labour market changes noted above, firm-level restructuring in recent years is often directly linked to the following labour market trends: (*i*) c anging occupational structure of employment; (*ii*) changing skill needs within existing occupations and industries; (*iii*) flexibility in forms of employment (e.g. casualisation, job sub-contracting, etc.) and (*iv*) flexi-pay system.

Given the compulsions and processes of adjustment, the deregulation and flexibility paradigm has assumed increasing significance, and interventions and regulations are being seen as creating distortions in various factor markets. Fallon a. id Lucas (1991) have used evidence from India and Zimbabwe to argue that job security regulations are associated with declining employment in the organised sector industries.[2] This shift in approach of the role of the public sector in the current affairs of economic management also has clear implications for skills development and training policies in an economy. For instance, on-the-job training, which in earlier decades was seen less prominently as a form of training, has emerged as an important new form of skills acquisition, and an instrument to keep the labour force flexible. In order to protect erosion of productivity, quality control and discontinuities, enterprises have shown an increasing tendency to

---

1. Cf. ILO, *Report on Wage Policy*, submitted to the Department of Labour and Employment, Government of Philippines, 1987.

2. For India, the study is based on observations of the impact of regulation as 35 industries. The long-term reduction in employment ranges from about 45 per cent in silk and synthetics to 0 per cent in textiles, tobacco and agricultural machineries.

promote on-the-job training, or retraining, and thus maintain the skills composition that is deemed optimal. As regards activities that come under sub-contracting and parcellisation, most of these require very few skills (e.g., assembly operations), which can be provided in-house with relative ease. This then is the changed scenario, carrying implications for manpower planning and skills development.

In the context of the surge towards privatisation, deregulation and restructuring, to what extent can manpower planning play a role in catering to changing occupation-specific skills requirements? The proponents of the MRA approach would tend to argue that shift of resources to 'targeted' industries would enhance demand for specific skills, which policy-makers should be able to forecast and aim to produce through education and training. Without such intervention, there may occur a shortage of 'critical' skills which may act as a deterrent to efficient restructuring. Further, private sector initiative in such skilling efforts may be inadequate owing to rigidities in the labour market as well as to the externalities attached to such training. These arguments are contested by the 'non-intervention' school who argue that the MRA is even more outmoded in view of the rapidity of firm-level changes, and the decline in the rate of growth of public sector employment. They further contend that both workers and employers have a mutual interest to participate in on-the-job training:

> A firm will be willing to invest in specific training with the intention of obtaining benefits in the form of more productive workers. Analogously, workers will be willing to make such investments if they obtain some of the return. Both employers and employees will share in the cost of investing and in the returns of specific training. After the training is complete, when employers and employees are earning 'profits' from the investment, they will be especially valuable to each other. Firms will be relatively unwillingly to lay off or fire workers in which they have made large investments; employees will be relatively unwilling to quit jobs in which they have made investments and are earning returns (Freeman, 1979).

The underlying theme of the non-intervention school is that the private sector will play an increasing role in job creation; that occupation-specific skills development should be left to firm-level training and fine-tuning; that the government should help enhance the employability of the work force by imparting flexible, broad-based education and training.[1]

There is hardly any doubt that there has started an irreversible trend toward reduced government sector role in employment and skills development, ostensibly owing as much to budgetary considerations as to limitations of human resource planning. The increasing deregulation, also extended to labour markets, carries in its sweep a diminishing significance of detailed and long-term manpower planning and skills development. Labour market analysis has taken on added significance and an active role in the changed scenario.

---

1. See Lucas (1991).

2.5   Labour Market Analysis as a Tool for HRD Planning

The strong emphasis, in the recent period, on replacing manpower planning through labour market analysis, is aptly captured in the following contention.

> As the keyword 'planning' is out, 'policy' and 'analysis' have become keywords that are in. Policy has more modest, short-term pretention than planning. Historically, manpower planners have locked themselves into long-term time horizons which leave little room for flexibility. In contrast, labour market analysts are constantly adjusting short and medium-term analyses to reflect changing conditions, while always keeping the long-term in mind (G. Psacharopoulos, 1991).

In the backdrop of the discussions in previous sections, especially on the limitations of manpower planning as a guide to educational and training policies as well as the increasing thrust of the private sector in employment and skills development, there are understandable reasons for advocating a diminished role for manpower planning. However, it is equally important to note that labour market analysis, as an alternative policy tool, has grown in significance owing to not only the fairly well-known limitations of manpower planning, but also a set of complex issues emanating from the advocacy and practice of a 'supply-side' economic policy framework. Such a policy framework, as observed earlier, is closely associated with labour market flexibilisation,[1] warranting, among other things, enterprise-oriented and enterprise-based skills development programmes.

Labour market analysis, by itself, is an ambivalent concept, and one needs to provide appropriate connotations and ingredients to it in order to make it relevant and operational. There is a whole range of issues that fall within the purview of labour market analysis, and one has to discern which ones are relevant to the economy's context. Recently there have been attempts at developing a labour market mode[2] that incorporates much more flexible assumptions than usually used in traditional manpower planning exercises. However, "even if such forecasting perfectly allows for the supply of skilled manpower required in the future, it cannot guarantee that optimal decisions are taken. Employees could, for various reasons, still be demanding a mix of manpower skills that was not socially optimal.[3] On the other hand, there exists sporadic empirical and conceptual work on examining how the labour market operates. These are related to specific objectives, and the scope is often dictated by the specific theme undertaken for investigation. Furthermore,

> now that the old manpower projections approach with which training planners used to work (but which didn't work!) has by and large been abandoned, *there seems to be a shortage of techniques and instruments which training policy-makers can employ with reasonable confidence.* Thus there appears

---

1. Cf. G. Standing (1991) for an exposition.
2. Cf. Hopkins et al., (1986); Cohen (1986).
3. ILO (1991).

to be a chasm between the sophisticated processes of labour market and employment planning on the one hand, and skills development provision on the other.[1]

Although the search for 'new' and 'alternative approaches' to manpower planning and analyses has started, there is very little in existing practice to sugges how, and to what extent, labour market analysis can actually *substitute* manpower planning in providing appropriate signals to overall human resource development planning. The neo-liberal paradigm (Psacharopoulos, 1991) often stems from assumptions of smooth markets, labour supply and demand functions and factor mobility, and hence misses out on empirically observed heterogeneity and imbalances in labour markets. The following are among several characteristics that strain the credibility of the neo-liberal approach.

(*i*)   Labour markets are often segmented for a variety of reasons, and the possibilities of labour market failures can have disastrous impact on labour. One must note here that labour cannot simply be seen as a 'commodity' or a simple factor of production.

(*ii*)   Small firms have a decisive disadvantage in promoting on-the-job training owing to scale of operations, and hence access to required skills could be facilitated by public sector vocational and training institutions.

(*iii*)   Structural adjustment has been observed to be associated with retrenchments as well as cuts in public expenditures, often leading to reduced incomes and employment opportunities for the poor. This has led the governments of many Asian countries to undertake 'social safety-net' programmes, including promotion of special employment schemes, income support and compensation. Training, too, has remained an important instrument of the government in their social targeting. In the event that structural adjustment and restructuring programmes fail to resume growth, training and human resource development will continue to be eminently a public concern as well.

There have been recent attempts to provide more pragmatic approaches. Godfrey (1991), for instance, offers a schematic approach that essentially dichotomises short- and long-run skills programmes, and combines current rate of analysis and analysis of expected structural change in the economy. His schematic approach involves (*i*) tracer studies of detailed, disaggregated samples of graduates; (*ii*) social and private costing of training, disaggregated at levels used in (*i*); (*iii*) calculations of internal rates of return; (*iv*) assessment of structural changes in the economy, to capture expanding and declining sectors and hence employment shares; (*v*) a comprehensive survey of employment of graduates in the various sectors/branches; and (*vi*) estimating changes in rates of return on various skills programmes due to changes in structure of the economy. While the above schema largely espouses the labour market approach, it implicitly takes recourse to some elements of manpower forecasts (structural changes and growth of sectors and employment), although detailed skills forecasts may not be called

---

1. D.L. Bowland (1992).

for. Moreover, the above schema, which appears to be a hybrid approach (combining MRA with LMA), would be more applicable to more organised skills development programmes and systems.

Notwithstanding the adequacy and comprehensiveness of labour market analysis as a tool for HRD planning, a core set of market issues which will need to be addressed and analysed, *inter alia*, would include the following:

(i)   Decisions on human resource development, employment and labour market policies cannot be divorced from the macro-economic policy framework and development objectives pursued by an economy. During the implementation of structural adjustment reforms, in-depth analysis and monitoring would be required to assess the employment and income effects of such reforms. Such analysis would provide important feedback to government policies on deregulation and flexibility as well as on providing safety nets, including special training and employment schemes.

(ii) A basic labour market issue common to most of the Asia-Pacific countries relates to the imbalances between labour supply and employment expansion. Employment growth in most of the labour surplus countries has slowed down during the 1980s, as compared to the 1970s, both in the agricultural sector and the organised manufacturing sector. If this trend continues, the informal sector may tend to expand and lower productivity. On the supply side, supply pressure in the labour market will continue in the next several years. Female participation in the labour force will continue to rise. Such imbalances will continue to challenge employment planners, and employment-intensive development may have to be designed to overcome such imbalances.

(iii) The question of employment generation cannot be addressed simply through aggregate estimations, but requires a rather detailed understanding and prognosis of the complex labour markets that exist in the rural and urban areas. An investigation into the nature of hierarchy of jobs, segmentation of markets, supply pressures and demand signals from labour markets, and the skills and mobility question will strengthen employment planning efforts. After all, planning employment, growth-induced or otherwise, has to be predicated on what kind of jobs need to be created, and for what kind of job-seekers. Given existing economic and institutional rigidities, it would be impossible to restructure labour markets and guarantee free access to, and mobility across, these markets. Nonetheless, labour market issues, properly identified and analysed, would be a crucial element in operationalising a full employment strategy.

(iv) At disaggregative levels too, the supply and demand imbalances will tend to be critical to labour market issues. As earlier mentioned, rapid expansion of tertiary education has often led to a severe surplus in unemployed graduates, and the after-effects of such a policy may be felt for quite some time in the future. In economies that are relatively slow-growing, educated unemployed poses a serious challenge. It is also significant to note that retrenchments and structural unemployment will further aggravate employment performance in the organised sector, especially if adjustment reforms proceed at a fast rate. Micro-level labour policy measures, which include employment service functions, training and retraining, would emerge as important labour market considerations.

(v) Firm-level restructuring, which is instrumental in a successful structural adjustment programme, needs to be understood and monitored closely. Unions and managements have different perceptions of adjustment and restructuring, and a consensus is required on major issues, such as voluntary retirement, retraining, redeployment, multi-skilling, etc. Successful firm-level adjustments need to be explored fully, which can help in negotiations. An important issue in this regard is to establish whether rising costs of firm production, that erode competitiveness, are due to rising labour compensation, to institutional bottlenecks or to tight labour market conditions.

(vi) In any labour market analysis, a study of wages would be central in many ways. Apart from its role in the overall framework of a labour market information system, wages would reflect real unit labour costs, i.e. competitiveness of industries and products, as well as reflect skill compensation. Movements in wage differentials would tend to reflect on skills differentials and signal potential mobility. It is also significant to analyse the impact of trade and exchange rate policies on wages, as well as the impact of wage patterns on the overall income distribution patterns in an economy.

(vii) The informal sector comprises rather wide array of activities, enterprises and work force. Viewing the informal sector from the labour market standpoint, one can identify the labour status of the work force, their vulnerability and work conditions (including the minimum wage question). Viewing the informal sector as an enterprise, one could ascertain the efficiency, productivity and employment-generating capabilities of the so-called micro-enterprise. Here, a distinct dualism could be discerned, with different implications for policy interventions. An in-depth profiling and desegregated analysis is required of this sector's employment and productivity. Planning technology upgradation and skills training for the sector, whether home-based, unskilled and/or casual, their employment/income situation needs to be evaluated properly, which will spell out disaggregated interventions as well.

To reiterate, there is nothing definitive about a labour market analysis framework, and the emerging labour market issues in any individual country will have to be examined in their own respective contexts.

2.6 Changing Role of Governments in HRD Planning

The labour market issues discussed above provide a broad contour of labour market concerns that can provide the necessary feedback to planners, including educational planners, to revise policies and programmes. One particular signal of this 'new approach' is that the government ought to rethink its time-honoured policies of expanding education and training with an open-ended objective of serving economic growth. Here, the role of public intervention is viewed with scepticism and should be confined to special circumstances and areas. For instance, the government could make use of labour market analyses for not only monitoring purposes, but also for dissemination in areas where information asymmetry exists. These analyses could also act as important guidelines in its overall macro-economic and sectoral policy exercises. Specific public interventions may however be called for when there are market failures; special social weights need to be provided (e.g., in the general literacy programme of the country) where private sector in skills development, owing to high costs and long gestation periods, may not be forthcoming and when human development concerns transcend simple business calculations of skills imbalances. Combining labour market analyses with its education and training policies would allow the government to reassess and revamp existing programmes and institutions (including vocational training), and reconsider decisions on subsidisation of education and skills development programmes. In short, what is being argued is that the public sector has to shift its role from creating and absorbing skills towards facilitating the creation and absorption of skills.

An area where the government can play a significant role within the labour market analysis framework, is in the labour market monitoring and information system. Since most of the developing countries suffer from market imperfections and information asymmetries leading to various imbalances and bottlenecks, the government would perhaps be in a superior position than the private sector to undertake to develop a labour market monitoring and information (LMI) system. The broad objective of this exercise would be to provide a nexus of 'information, analysis and action[1] for the efficient utilisation of human resources. While the government's role in the areas of 'information' building and labour market 'analysis' is clear, the nature of 'action' has to be rationalised in the context of the imbalances that need to be redressed. Such action need not be in the labour market itself, since, for example, increasing labour demand to resolve excess supply would lie, well beyond the labour market, in the patterns of economic growth.[2]

In the changing economic environment discussed above, with rapid reforms taking place in the fields of trade, public expenditure, financial and labour markets, LMI and labour market analysis assume an important role in guiding the overall employment and manpower situation in the economy. For instance, redeployment of workers declared redundant during an industrial restructuring process not only requires a basic information system to monitor their numbers and the patterns of skills they possess, but also to analyse and plan to guide them for retraining and relocation in different lines of production that are emerging. Recently, in India, sweeping reforms have been introduced as part of a structural adjustment programme. Preliminary studies indicate that these reforms, in the

---

1. Cf. Papola (1991).
2. Ibid.

short- to medium-term, may not only cause widespread redundancies but also create large additional unemployment, especially in the informal non-agricultural sector. A close examination and monitoring of the employment/income effects of these reforms are called for, so that policy measures and programmes could be attuned to mitigate such adverse consequences.

The LMI and labour market analysis, therefore, can act as an extremely useful and forceful guide to employment and skills planning in an economy. Concerted efforts would be required to build up an appropriate monitoring and information system that can provide, to the policy-planners, practitioners and the private sector, accurate and unambiguous information and understanding of labour market processes.

The role of the government in the areas outlined above essentially involves manpower analysis, as opposed to traditional manpower planning, which is precisely what the proponenets of LMA would propose. The government is seen as "a collector and provider of information, a facilitator, an identifier of problems, an appraiser, an evaluator, and a nudger of institutions with long lead times in desirable directions."[1] The question, here, is whether the above description of the role of government in HRD planning is commensurate with the tasks and challenges confronted by governments in the developing countries. Is 'lesser government' a panacea to the state of literacy and levels of human development in these countries? Has this been the case with the Asian NIEs, whom many other countries are trying to emulate?[2]

It is pertinent to note that while the market approach has surely started affecting policy environment in the developing world, there is also a renewed pledge on the role of governments to invest in education and other social infrastructure, ostensibly in recognition of the imperfections in markets to cater to equity, poverty alleviation and human resource development. In point of fact, in the backdrop of experiences of structural adjustment during the 1980s, targeting of social programmes including training 'as a complement to equity strategies',[3] are being increasingly advocated to cushion adverse impact on social indicators. The role of governments would thus continue to be of crucial significance in several areas, as mentioned earlier, where alternatives are less forthcoming, or where markets tend to fail and the constraints are of a structural nature.

2.7 In Lieu of Conclusions

This paper has sought to underscore the significance of HRD planning in the process of economic transformation of developing countries. However, in the

---

1. Cf. Godfrey (1991).

2. It is contended that "in these countries the governments carried through extensive education programmes to create an effective and responsive labour force; they provided adequate and well-administered infrastructure in the form of energy and transport facilities so that shortages of these inputs have not been bottlenecks to industry; they provided stable legal frameworks for private activity in a market environment; and established conditions for the smooth functioning of factor markets for capital and labour, in addition to product markets." (Quoted from G. Rosen's lecture at the Asian Development Bank's Distinguished Speakers Programme, *ADB Quarterly Review*, January 1992.)

3. Cf. World Bank (1991).

recent period, especially during the adjustment decade of the 1980s, the role of government, public institutions and 'planning' in the process of adjustment and growth is being reassessed. Manpower planning which has hitherto been an integral element of HRD planning has been attacked from various empirical and conceptual standpoints. Here, the criticisms have been addressed largely to the MRA or forecasting exercise of manpower planning where skills and occupational categories are projected to assess and resolve demand-supply imbalances. Given the increasing scepticism on the reliability of such an approach, a new approach based on labour market analysis is being forwarded. This approach has gained increasing attention in recent years with the increasing significance of the 'neo-liberal' paradigm that calls for greater privatisation, the reduced role of government as custodian of public concerns including job creation, and a deregulated and flexible labour market. In the context of education and skills development, planning should be seen as a 'facilitating' and not an 'intervention' exercise.

The labour market analysis approach is unquestionably important in attempting to capture appropriate labour market signals based on which training and skills programmes can be modified. The approach is, however, eclectic and there is no unique method of analysing labour markets. Moreover, labour market analysis would not be able to capture the entire spectrum of HRD planning, which goes beyond private cost-benefit analysis in education and skills development.

It has been argued that in the developing countries, state intervention will have to continue in the area of HRD planning, on grounds of efficiency as well as equity.[1] It has to be noted that manpower and educational planning, as part of HRD planning, would have to be seen as a continuous process, and not discretely and discontinuously as done by the MRA approach. Efficiency in investment on education and training which requires that the demand-supply imbalance be minimised, would have to be guided not only by the rate of return approach (which also has its conceptual and measurement difficulties), but also by extensive manpower and labour market analysis. To what extent such state interventions are necessary, and what shape these will take would have to be country-specific, and are outside the scope of this paper.[2]

There is hardly any country which can be appropriately singled out as having successfully pursued a HRD-led growth policy. Several authors have attempted to show the Republic of Korea as a recent example where deliberate policies towards education and skilling have helped lay the foundations of high-tech growth. This association, as mentioned earlier, cannot be taken as a causal explanation, since other examples such as Sri Lanka and the Philippines, with high educational attainments, would tend to contradict it. Yet, despite the lack of established evidence between HRD and growth,[3] human resource planning will continue to be pursued not only on social considerations, but also to provide a strong and basic foundation to the country's skill force.

---

1. See Lucas (1991) for some of the arguments in favour of such interventions.
2. See Godfrey (1991) for an 'alternative approach'.
3. Behrman (1990).

While the debate on the manpower planning approach versus labour market approach continues, it is important to ask how far HRD planning can be predicated on the strengths of one or the other. After all, the human resource planning of a country is a deeper economic and social concern than can possibly be captured within the individual framewc⁻ks of the two approaches.

References

Amjad, Rashid (ed.), 1987. *Human Resource Planning : The Asian Experience*, ILO-ARTEP, New Delhi.

Asian Development Bank, 1990. *Human Resource Policy and Economic Development : Selected Country Studies.*

Becker, Gary S., 1967. 'Human Capital and the Personal Distribution of Income: An Analytical Approach', Woytinsky Lecture. University of Michigan, Republished in Gary S. Becker, *Human Capital*, 2nd edition, NBER, New York, 1975, 94–117.

Behrman J., 1990. *Human Resource-Led Development : Review of Issues and Evidence*, ILO-ARTEP.

Bowland, D.L., 1992. Current Issues in the Reform of Training Systems : An Agenda for Discu. .ion' (mimeo.).

Cohen, S. I. (1986). "Developments in the Analysis and Planning of Labour and Manpower", WEP Working Paper, ILO, Geneva.

Colclough, C., 1990. How can the manpower planning debate be resolved', in R. Amjad *et al., Quantitative Techniques in Employment Planning.*

Debeauvais and G. Psacharopoulos, 1985. 'Forecasting the Needs for Qualified Manpower: Towards an Evaluation', in Hinchliffe and R. Yondi (eds), *Forecasting Skilled Manpower Needs: The Experience of Eleven Countries*, UNESCO, Paris.

Fallon, P.R. and R.E. Lucas, 1991. 'The Impact of Changes in Job Security Regulations in India and Zimbabwe', *World Bank Economic Review*, Vol. 5, No.3.

Fong, Pang Eng, 1982. *Education, Manpower and Development in Singapore*, Singapore.

Freeman, R.B. 1979. *Labour Economics*, 2nd edition, Prentice-Hall, Englewood Cliffs, N.J.

Godfrey, Martin, 1991. 'Education, Training and Employment : What Can Planners Do?', Paper presented at ILO-ARTEP's Employment Planners' Meeting, 17–19 December 1991.

Hollister, R.G., 1981. The Relevance of Manpower Planning in a Rapidly Expanding Economy (mimeo).

Hopkins, Michael et. al. (1986). "MACBETH: A Model for Forecasting Population, Education, Manpower, Employment, Underemployment and Unemployment, WEP Working Paper, ILO, Geneva.

ILO-ARTEP, 1984. *Employment and Manpower Planning: A Manual for Training in Basic Techniques*, Bangkok.

ILO, 1991. Manpower Planning and Analysis : An Issues Paper (mimeo.), Geneva.

Islam, I., 1989. 'Industrial Restructuring and Industrial Relations in ASEAN : A Firm-Level Chronicle', in G. Edgren (ed.), *Restructuring, Employment and Industrial Relations*, ILO-ARTEP, New Delhi.

Krause, Lawrence B., 1989. Issues of Macro-Adjustment Affecting Human Resource Development in Malaysia : A Human Resource Strategy (mimeo.).

Lucas, Robert E., 1988. 'On the Mechanics of Economic Development', *Journal of Monetary Economics*, 21, 3–42.

Lucas, Robert E., 1991. Manpower Planning and Economic Development (mimeo.).

Lucas, Robert E. and Don Verry, 1989. Human Resource Development Project : Draft Final Report (mimeo.), Malaysian EPU/UNDP/ILO-ARTEP Project.

Otani, I. and D. Villanueva, 1989. 'Major Determinants of Long-Term Growth in LDCs', *Finance and Development*, September.

Papola, T.S. 1991. Labour Market Monitoring for Employment Planning (mimeo.).

Planning Commission, Government of India, "Towards Social Transformation: Approach to the Eighth Five Year Plan 1990-95", (mimeo), May 1990.

Psacharopoulos, George (1991). "From Manpower Planning to Labour Market Analysis", *International Labour Review*, Vol. 130, No. 4, pp. 459-470

Psacharopoulos, George and A.M. Arriagada 1986. 'The Educational Composition of the Labour Force : An International Comparison', *International Labour Review*, Vol. 125, No. 5, September–October.

Rodgers, G., 1990. 'Labour market modelling and employment and manpower planning techniques', in Rashid Amjad *et al.*, op. cit.

Roe, Alan R., 1984. 'Industrial Restructuring : Issues and Experiences in Selected Developed Economies, World Bank Technical Paper No. 21.

Schultz, T.W., 1962. 'Reflections on Investment in Man', *The Journal of Political Economy*, Vol. LXX No. 5, Part 2, October.

Singer, H.W. and N.D. Baster, 1980. *Youth Human Resources in Korea's Social Development*, KDI.

Standing, Guy (1991). "The Labour Impact of Technological Change in a Developing Country: An Empirical Approach", WEP Working Paper, ILO, Geneva.

Sussangkorn, Chalongphob, 1991. Thai Economic Growth, Emerging Labour Market Problems and Policy Responses (mimeo).

Thamarajakshi, R., 1988. *Human Resource Development in Asian Countries: An Integrated Approach*, HRD Working Paper, ILO-ARTEP, New Delhi.

World Bank, 1991. 'Vocational and Technical Education and Training', Policy Paper.

Discussion

The principal discussant, Dr T.S. Papola, Adviser, Planning Commission, Government of India, recapitulated the salient features of Dr Muqtada's paper and added his viewpoint on the limitations of both the manpower requirements approach (MRA) and the manpower planning approach (MPA). He stressed that HRD planning was the most comprehensive as it encompasses both the development and utilisation of human resources. When skill requirements change rapidly then MRA becomes redundant as it is more suitable for longer-term solutions. He then went on to examine the role of the state in building capacities through institutional training. While the role of state was predominant for planning the development of higher level manpower, the role of industry would have to increase in the area of on-the-job training and production in order to maximise outputs.

A participant from India raised the question as to whether adjustment can really be painless in areas of skill formation, in particular, in the unorganised sector where new technologies have destabilising effects. He stressed the need for state intervention as enterprises are not always equipped with the wherewithal to cope with changes in skill requirements. New information-based technologies must be less workshop-oriented and more based on the classroom approach. Therefore, if skill levels have to be raised, curricula need to be changed at the school level.

The participant from Pakistan pointed out that it was wrong to suggest that there exists only an association between economic growth and HRD and not a strong causal relationship between human capital and growth. He quoted the examples of Sri Lanka and Philippines where without economic stability there has been no growth whereas in Japan HRD has been a necessary condition for growth.

The representative from Nepal observed that MRA is a good approach at the policy level but at the operational level it has limitations.

A Bangladesh delegate pointed to data inadequacies in most developing countries and the need to overcome this problem if HRD indicators are monitored.

The participant from Lao PDR commented that the labour market approach is inadequate in so far as it fails to cover the informal sector. Labour market information, in order to give a realistic picture, must provide insights on this sector.

The employers' representative from Pakistan objected to the use of the word 'manpower' and suggested that 'human power' be used. He also pointed that some of the statistics represented in Table 1 of the paper were not relevant as they related to the early 1960s for certain countries. He also stated that all planning processes can be thrown out of gear if the countries concerned face the problem of unchecked population growth. The government was not playing a major role in

Pakistan vis-à-vis training and it was the private enterprises who had a major role to play. The government should come up with practical suggestions for training and self-employment.

The r ꞓresentative from Malaysia reiterated the earlier observation, stating that the government has to provide guidance to training and educational institutions and pay special attention to neglected sectors in Malaysia which are undergoing a process of rapid privatisation. Another representative from Malaysia pointed to the limitations of MRA as in many economies the labour market information system was not developed enough to support any analysis of the labour market. He observed that education and training can be controlled by employers to the extent that they can influence curriculum development as they provide direct inputs. The government's role should be restricted to a regulatory one in terms of setting standards, legislation and policy but not implementation.

Dr Muqtada, responding to the comments, made the following observations. He pointed out that MPA and LMA are not mutually exclusive. A mix of both is often necessary and their relative roles change with labour market conditions in different countries. The answer lies in arriving at a balanced HRD strategy which takes into consideration the roles of government and private enterprises to build capabilities. In the context of changing economies of Asia which experience a rise of on-the-job training, the training systems require revamping to keep pace with new industry specific needs. HRD planning must be in agreement with social concerns for human development and non-economic factors may be used for segmentation of the labour market. Government intervention to make this change as painless as possible is crucial.

3

Education, Training and Employment: What Can Planners Do?[1]

MARTIN GODFREY

3.1 Introduction

It is little short of amazing that, after more than a quarter of a century, the controversy over the manpower requirements approach to human resource development planning is still alive, but it seems to be so. Indeed, in recent years, with the advent of a "new" approach to manpower analysis, the dispute seems to have been revived. Ironically, as most academics working in the field have come to the view that the manpower requirements methodology is totally discredited, its popularity with policy-makers has never been greater.

One reason for the failure of theorists to convince the practitioners may be that their criticisms were too destructive. So appalling were the defects of the methodology, they appeared to argue, the forecasts based on it should play no role at all in the planning process. The mission to rid the world of forecasting was always impossible. It may even have reinforced the tenacity with which manpower planners stuck to the methodology. It is more realistic to assume that, however much the purists may deplore it, planners will continue to use the manpower requirements approach. In which case it may be useful to try to define the limits of what it can be used for, in terms that are sufficiently practical to be convincing to planners.

With this purpose in mind, this paper starts with a brief description of the approach and a summary of economists' criticisms of it. Then an attempt is made to define what questions it can (and cannot) help planners to answer. Finally, the question is addressed: if not forecasting, what can planners of education, training and employment most usefully do?

3.2 The Manpower Requirements Approach

The term 'manpower requirements approach' defines a method of projecting an economy's demand for manpower by educational and occupational category, for

---

1. This paper briefly summarises the argument of the book of the same title, recently published by ILO-ARTEP (Godfrey, 1991), and further develops its conclusions.

comparison with projections of supply, more or less as follows. (Variations in methodology exist but do not, on the whole, affect its logic).

(1)   The first step is to disaggregate gross domestic product (GDP) by sector in the base year.

(2)   Next, the number employed in each occupational category is added to the number of 'vacancies' to give a figure for the stock of workers in that category 'demanded' by each sector in the base year.

(3)   Targets are set for growth of GDP by sector or realistic assumptions are made about likely sectoral growth rates over the planning period.

(4)   Assumptions are made, on the basis of either past experience or international cross-section regressions, about the likely growth rate of productivity of each occupation in each sector.

(5)   Subtracting these category-specific productivity growth rates from the sectoral GDP growth rates yields a figure for rate of growth of demand for each category due to economic growth.

(6)   The increase in demand due to replacement of (a) non-citizens, (b) wastage due to death, retirement and other forms of separation from the labour force, and (c) net emigrants, is then added in, to give the total increase in demand (or demand for new entrants) for each occupational category.

(7)   Finally on the demand side, the figures for increase in demand by occupational category are converted into figures for increase in demand by educational levels, by means of an occupation/education matrix, reflecting either the actual pattern in the base-year or the planners' assumptions about how the educational requirements for each occupation will change over the period.

On the supply side, an estimate is then made of the numbers likely to join the labour force over the same period, (a) by educational qualification and (b) by occupation/skill level. A comparison of demand and supply projections yields estimates of 'shortages' and 'surpluses' over the period. The pattern of shortages is usually taken as an indicator of the detailed 'training needs' of the economy.

3.3   The Economists' Critique

The criticisms of the manpower requirements approach made by economists are so familiar as to scarcely need repeating. Substitutability, between labour and other factors, between workers of different educational levels within occupations, and between occupations, is assumed to be zero; variations in cost of schooling and training, in wages and in prices of all kinds are assumed to have no effect on coefficients in the manpower forecasting formula. Observed coefficients, on which targets or growth paths are based, are assumed to be optimal. Etc.

Protestations that the real world is not like this cut little ice with planners who routinely use fixed-coefficient input-output models to project output by sector and industry. More recently the critique has become more practical and thus potentially more effective. An important factor here has been the advent of a 'new approach' to manpower planning, advocated by a number of authors in a

World Bank Staff Working Paper (Psacharopoulos *et al.*, 1983) and, more recently, at an Orientation on Manpower Planning in Jakarta in July 1986 (Indonesian Manpower Management Information System, 1986).

The main burden of their critique is that forecasts based on the manpower requirements approach are neither accurate nor necessary. Their inaccuracy, reflecting the poverty of the data used, the weaknesses of the methodology and the inherent uncertainty of the future (Dougherty, 1983), has been demonstrated by evaluations of a wide range of forecasts (Hollister, 1967; Jolly and Colclough, 1972; Ahamad and Blaug, 1973; Amjad, 1985; Youdi and Hinchliffe, 1985).

The lack of need for manpower projections of the usual kind is argued on several grounds. Hasibuan (1986) argues that "there are strong indications to show that organisations with a fairly functioning feedback system could and did identify shortages and took effective action to overcome them". The possibility of such action, including on-the-job and in-service training and importation of manpower from abroad, means that "shortage of manpower is not of crucial concern".

Hasibuan points out that formal education and training are not the only source of skills, which are acquired also in the home, in enterprises and through adult education. Clark (1986) also points to the existence of many other sources of training and skills development besides government training programmes, as does Dougherty (1983, 1986) who regards it as "unlikely that the Manpower Development Planning Unit will be able to monitor (such sources) directly to any great extent, never mind make quantitative recommendations concerning the extent of its provision." Dougherty (1986) draws particular attention to the (often neglected) transfer of skills from abroad through training by multinational corporations and overseas partners in joint enterprises, by overseas firms under licensing agreements and by suppliers of equipment. He expresses the hope that parts of the manpower development sector can be made self-regulating, so that planners can concentrate their efforts on the remainder.

Hollister (1983, 1986) adds the point that the concern with 'critical shortages' is only relevant where the gestation period for training is long and expensive. Eighty to ninety per cent of manpower in this category is employed in the public sector. So for most types of manpower long-term projections are unnecessary (since additions to the stock can be made quickly). And, even where such projections are useful, they need concern only the public sector rather than the economy as a whole. Dougherty (1983) similarly allows a role for forecasting only in the case of occupations where demand can be related to demographic, social or political norms, such as teachers, doctors, nurses and the police.

A virtually lone voice at the Jakarta orientation in favour of economy-wide forecasts of manpower requirements was that of Cohen (1986). He describes such forecasts as

> an essential input for the analysis and planning of global magnitudes with respect to the development and utilisation of human resources in the medium run.... For many decisions at cabinet level and/or minister level, policy-making requires reliable forecasts about probable trends in the future....(including) the development and employment of manpower. To ridicule such forecasts and the models behind them betrays little acquaintance with policy-making at higher levels of decision-making.

It is certainly true that decision-makers at these higher levels still want forecasts—to the exasperation of critics of this approach. Having demonstrated that "making long-term projections of manpower supply and demand on the basis of general economy-wide planning methods is not likely to be a very fruitful enterprise for a developing country". Hollister (1983) has to recognise that, "unfortunately, in many developing countries this is precisely the activity which has taken up most of the time and resources of manpower planning groups." Dougherty (1983) glumly concedes that "the view that planning consists of the preparation of detailed forecasts of supply and demand may be deeply entrenched even where the approach is patently impracticable". Amjad (1985) observes that precise quantitative projections "have little bearing on actual policy implementation but the demand to generate them has in no way decreased over the years." Indeed their popularity may have increased since the early 1970s: "the critical bombardment appears to have had no effect on practitioners' use of the approach and more and more countries have in fact adopted it", even though "individuals in manpower development units are sometimes almost apologetic about their forecasting work" (Psacharopoulos and Hinchliffe, 1983). Seven out of ten market economies covered by a recent review of Asian experience in human resource planning have used the manpower forecasting approach (Amjad, 1987). Ironically, the World Bank may have helped to encourage the survival of the methodology since, at least until a recent change of heart. "most requests for education loans from the World Bank and most project appraisals" have been "justified on the grounds of manpower requirements" (Psacharopoulos and Woodhall, 1985: 77).

However, the undoubted resilience of high-level demand for forecasts does not excuse human resource development planners from their professional duty to point out what they can and cannot be used for and to draw political decision-makers' attention to more useful and cost-effective techniques where they exist.

3.4 The Limitation of Data Inadequacies

Even if the conceptual criticisms of the methodology are disregarded and it is accepted on its own terms, manpower projections cannot be used to derive an economy's training needs, for several practical reasons.

(1) The first is the poor quality of occupational data. For instance, 64 per cent of those categorised in Indonesia's 1980 census (used as a base for several projections) as physical scientists and related technicians had primary schooling or less!

(2) Even if the data were of perfect quality, they are too highly aggregated. Even disaggregation to the three-digit level (nearly 300 categories in ISCO) lumps together occupations with very different training requirements.

(3) Even if the occupational categories could be sufficiently disaggregated, occupation is not the same thing as skill level. Statistically generalisable surveys cannot, in their nature, capture the extent to which those classified in a particular occupation (even if accurately so) are able to

perform competently. In which case the use of the total number in an occupational category as the base for projecting the demand for trained workers in this category could be grossly misleading.

(4) Even if comprehensive information about the capacities of the base-date work force were available, to decide whether *new* training programmes were needed it would be necessary to know all about *existing* training programmes. As already emphasised, this does not mean only government training programmes, which may indeed represent only a small proportion of total training, in comparison with on-the-job and off-the-job training by companies, private training institutions, licensors, suppliers of equipment, etc. To collect comprehensive and up-to-date information about government training programmes alone would be difficult enough. For private training institutions it would be more difficult still; for instance, even the number of private universities in Indonesia (well over 500) is not exactly known. In the case of company training, training by equipment suppliers, etc., it would be virtually impossible. *But if you don't know what you've got how do you know what you need?*

In short, even if the conceptual objections to the methodology are waived, and it is accepted in its own terms, there is simply not enough information to enable manpower projections to be used to derive occupational training needs. It is actually dishonest to pretend otherwise, however much high-level decision-makers may be clamouring for such figures.

3.5 The Limits of the Manpower Requirements Approach

What, then, can be done with projections based on the manpower requirements approach? The answer is: "not much, but a little."

A supply-side model alone can be used in some simple simulations to estimate the impact on numbers joining the labour force of various changes in policy, such as variations in repetition rates, in drop-out rates or in rates of transition from one level of the school system to another, or changes in the output/enrolment ratio at university level or in labour force participation rates. An exercise along these lines for Indonesia (Godfrey, 1991: Ch. 3) shows that the *easiest* way of keeping potential job-seekers off the streets (i.e. reducing the numbers joining the labour force) is to increase repetition rates by tightening up the rules for progression from one grade to another in primary schools. For instance, an increase in the repetition rate to 20 per cent would have cut the number joining the labour force in 1987-93 by 133 per cent.

There are several things missing from analysis of this kind, however. One is *cost*. There may be cheaper ways of keeping young people off the streets than retaining them in primary school—for instance, non-formal educational courses. Another consideration is *educational efficiency*. Some ways of retaining youngsters in schools may be more efficient educationally than others: reducing primary school drop-out to zero has a similar effect on labour supply at a similar cost to increasing repetition rates to 20 per cent but is preferable on grounds of educational efficiency. A final omission from the analysis is any consideration of *labour market outcome.* Some ways of reducing labour supply have a more beneficial impact on future productivity than others: for instance, rescuing drop-outs from illiteracy and innumeracy is likely to yield higher returns than imparting technical skills which will be quickly forgotten and never used.

Projections of both demand and supply can be used, also, along similiar lines to ILO-sponsored research of fifteen years ago on the "basic arithmetic of youth employment, education and unemployment" (Dore *et al.* 1976), to illustrate the scale of adjustment that might be needed in a labour market to increased output from the education system. An exercise along these lines for Indonesia (Godfrey, 1991: Ch. 2), for instance, forecasts, on plausible assumptions about the pace and pattern of economic growth and about output from the educational system, huge 'surpluses' of secondary school-leavers. In other words, by 1993 senior secondary school-leavers will be doing jobs held by primary or junior secondary school-leavers in 1980, and junior secondary school-leavers will be doing jobs previously held by those with less than complete primary schooling.

The results of projections of this kind are not easy for planners to interpret. Do huge 'surpluses' mean (as early manpower planners might have suggested) that the rate of expansion of schooling ought to be slowed down? Do the supply-side simulations discussed earlier mean that resources should be expended on keeping potential job-seekers off the streets, either by retaining them in the school system or by laying on post-school training courses for them?

Further information would be needed to take decisions of this kind. In particular we would need to know more about the impact of educational expansion on rates of return and about the costs and benefits of the various ways of reducing labour supply. Qualifications escalation, along with the growth of educated unemployment, is likely to involve a fall in such rates but not necessarily to a level that makes education a bad investment. In the absence of this further information the most that can be derived from projections of this kind is an idea of the scale of adjustment that is likely to be needed in the labour market. And the only policy implication is the apparently rather lame one of ensuring that the adjustment to changing labour market conditions is as smooth as possible, by providing accurate and up-to-date information to teachers, trainers, students, parents and employers. In short, "not much, but a little" can be learned from such projections.

3.6   The New Approach to Manpower Planning

If this represents the limit of what can be achieved by the manpower requirements approach, such projections and simulations are likely to represent only a small part of the work of manpower planners. How should they spend the rest of their working time? The message of the advocates of the 'new approach' to manpower planning is that they should learn as much as possible about the working of labour markets and the differing processes of entry into the workforce, advancement and skill acquisition in the various sectors.

The purpose of acquiring such knowledge would be to guide decisions about priorities for investment (and disinvestment) in education (of which government is likely to remain the main provider) and to optimise government interventions in the field of training. Such interventions should aim, as far as possible, to make the training system self-regulating, with decisions about content and quality in the hands of employers, and manpower planners playing a facilitating role.

The criteria for investment and disinvestment decisions would be labour market outcomes in relation to cost. These may be embodied in rate-of-return calculations, although the limitations of such calculations are recognised and they are regarded as only a first-stage screen.

Projections would only be used for the public sector, which employs virtually all the manpower for which the gestation period for training is long and expensive, and then mainly for occupations where demand can be related to demographic, social or political norms. Interview-surveys (to throw light on labour market processes) and tracer studies would be the main activities.

Long-term economy-wide projections are not seen as necessary for planning for the introduction of new skills which is likely to be demand-driven rather than supply-driven (in contrast, say, to the case of small-scale agriculture). It can thus be left largely to employers and trainers, with planners playing only a coordinating role. Quality of education (and the consequent capacity to innovate and adapt) is regarded as more important for the introduction of new types of skill than the prior existence of particular occupational categories. The transfer of new skills from abroad (more important than is generally realised) needs to be nurtured by planners rather than discouraged.

How helpful are these suggestions for a new agenda for human resource development planners?

Their emphasis looks entirely right, but the struggle to transform the real world into the ideal context for the new approach (a largely self-regulating, privatised training system) may not be so easy. Pre-career, out-of-plant training programmes for school-leavers, though expensive, tend to be popular with governments in countries where the rate of increase of school outputs exceeds that of new jobs. Expansion of such programmes can ease, at least temporarily, the problem of educated unemployment.

3.7 An Alternative Approach to Analysis of Future Directions

Thus manpower planners are probably going to have to live with the continued existence of a fair number of pre-career government training institutions and will probably still have to advise on the nature of the programmes that they should run. How they should approach this depends largely on the length of the programmes on offer and the consequent leadtime necessary for the implementation of changes in them.

In the case of short programmes, to a large extent planning can be handed over to those who run them. This involves making training institutions more flexible and more responsive to the changing situation in local labour markets by devolving decision-making and financial responsibility to managers of such institutions and involving local employers in their design, management and finance. This alone should ensure that training programmes are relevant to the current needs of the local economy, but occasional appraisal, monitoring and evaluation through cost/outcome analysis may also be useful.

For programmes with long lead-times, however, cost/outcome analysis alone, based on the current state of the labour market, may be a misleading guide for planners' decisions. Structural changes in the economy may alter the social profitability of long courses by the time their graduates emerge. An alternative approach to the analysis of future directions needs to be devised, combining (*a*) current rate-of-return analysis and (*b*) analysis of expected structural change in the economy.

The focus of this alternative approach would be not on occupation but on type of educational or training qualification. This is partly because, as already discussed, of all the statistics handled by labour economists, those concerning occupation are of the poorest quality. It could also be argued that technological change is undermining the very concept of occupation, at least in manufacturing. Correspondence between academic specialisation and eventual occupation is far from complete. And, after all, what counts for the external efficiency of a training programme is its impact on the productivity of those who go through it; the occupations that they end up in matter, for planning purposes, only in so far as they affect their productivity.

The alternative approach would have six steps as follows.

(*a*)   The first step would be a *tracer study* of a sample of graduates of the programme in question. Useful lessons can be learned from international experience in this field (e.g., from Statistics Canada, 1989; Sanyal *et al.*, 1987; Arcelo and Sanyal, 1987; Mehmet and Yip, 1986). For instance, separate cohorts should be separately sampled; a jumble of graduates over a long period is unlikely to be representative of every cohort. Disaggregation by field of study and type of qualification needs to be as detailed as possible. This suggests a need for a large sample, at least enough to ensure analysable answers by detailed field of study. It is also important to achieve a high response rate, to ensure that respondents are representative. However, questionnaires do not need to be long. In particular, we are interested not in graduates' opinions, attitudes, motives, job satisfaction, etc., but only in what has happened to them (including their remuneration).

(*b*)   Analysis of the *cost* of the courses would be the next step, based on information about *private cost* obtained from graduates and data on expenditure of the training institution that could be used for *social cost* calculations. Cost data would need to be disaggregated to the same level of detail as that used in the tracer study.

(*c*)   The results of the tracer study and the cost estimates could then be embodied in calculations of the internal *rate of return* (private and social) on each type of course in the usual way.

(*d*)   The fourth step would be to build up as detailed a picture as possible of likely *structural changes* in the economy over the planning period. The particular aim would be to identify sectors and branches which are likely to decline relatively, in employment terms, and those which are likely to increase in relative importance (including branches which do not at present exist in the economy in any substantial way).

(e)   Fifth, a comprehensive *survey of employment of graduates* of the courses under review would be mounted. The data to be collected from each of the sectors/branches surveyed would include the detailed educational qualification, by field of study, level and institution, of each graduate employee, and the number of such employees as a proportion of total employment in that branch.

In the case of sectors and branches which do not yet exist in the country in any substantial way or in which rapid technological change is in prospect, it would be useful to collect data, at a similar level of detail, from another economy at a more advanced level of development. The idea here would not be to use the pattern of employment in the higher-income economy as a 'target' for the lower-income economy in such sectors and branches. This would be misleading since the optimum degree of 'graduate-intensiveness' in any sector and any country will depend on, among other things, salary levels and differentials in that country. Thus data would need to be collected on graduate employment not only in the 'new' sector in the comparator country but also in some of the older industries in that country, with a view to assessing the *relative* graduate-intensity of the sector/branch in question and the *difference* in the *pattern* of graduate employment.

(f)   Finally, the data collected on expected structural change in the economy would be used to estimate what is likely to happen to rates of return on each specialisation.

In the case of demand for graduates in the *government services sector* a detailed projection of demand should be possible. In many cases (e.g., teachers, doctors, nurses, police) a first set of targets by occupation could be related to demographic, social or political norms. However, actual demand will be constrained by revenue possibilities (and it is *demand* rather than targets which is of interest here), so projections of government revenue and current expenditure would form the framework for this exercise. Moreover, figures on demand by occupational category would have to be translated into demand by academic specialisation (reflecting desired increases in hiring standards) before conclusions could be drawn about the likely impact on patterns of rates of return of changes in the government services sector.

In the *rest of the economy* the main focus of interest would be on the more volatile and graduate-intensive sectors. Data collected on these and other sectors would enable a judgement to be reached about the direction of the likely net effect of structural change on rates of return by academic specialisation. For instance, if a relative decline in the crude oil and natural gas sector and a relative increase in the importance of the communication equipment sector were expected, this might be expected to reduce rates of return on mining engineering and geology degrees and increase them on electronic engineering degrees. The implications of changing the assumptions about the nature of structural changes could be explored.

The end-product of all this would be a Table showing the best estimate of the current rate of return (social and private) on each qualification (by specialisation, level, etc.), the direction of change in that rate that would be expected over the planning period if the rate at which the stock was growing remained unchanged, and the reasons for that expectation (e.g., "government demand stagnant, net decline in other sectors").

Conceptual problems do, of course, arise in the use of earnings as a measure of benefit in calculations of social rate of return (for further discussion see Hunting, Zymelman and Godfrey, 1986). These mean that planners who follow this alternative approach have to use their informed judgement in deciding in which direction and roughly by how much their estimates of social rates of return on the programmes under review need to be modified. They have to get out of their offices and develop a 'feel' for the relevant training programmes and labour markets by keeping in touch with educators, trainers, employers, employees, trainees, job-seekers and observers. They also have to become knowledgeable about trends in technology and international product markets which will affect the future structure of the economy. And, in contrast to most manpower forecasting which aims at a one-off report, this has to be a continuous process; indicators have to be constantly updated as new information becomes available about rates of return and expected structural change. Clark (1986:138) calls it "an evolving procedure whereby appropriate and timely advice is constantly being fed into decision making about education and training. The advice will change as new information becomes available, economic conditions change, or objectives are modified".

A final advantage of this approach is that non-economic factors (not captured by rates of return) can easily be brought into the analysis. For instance, a government might decide that, in spite of a low current and prospective rate of return on training of architects, it wants to build up a School of Islamic Architecture. The planners' responsibility in this case would be to point to the need to do something about the low private rate of return, for instance, by commissioning the services of such architects, in order to attract good students who might otherwise choose other courses. In general, also, the approach draws attention to the cost, in terms of the higher rate of return foregone on other courses, of deciding to expand a programme purely on political grounds.

3.8   Conclusions

The idea of the planner as setter of precise targets was, in most countries, always something of a delusion; such targets, mercifully in view of their tenuous basis, have bad very little influence on events. The role of the planner in the alternative approach outlined in this paper is more realistic—a collector and provider of information, a facilitator, an identifier of problems, an appraiser, an evaluator, and a nudger of institutions with long lead-times in desirable directions.

In the case of short courses, the emphasis would be on setting up structures and processes which ensured relevance and efficiency, putting training institutions virtually on automatic pilot. Such monitoring as might be required could largely be devolved to the institutions themselves. In the case of long courses, the statistical task might be described as the collection of data of high quality about a small part of the training system and labour market, in contrast to the manpower forecasters' practice of relying on data of poor quality abut the whole of the labour market and as much of the training system as they could find. Undoubtedly, particularly in the early stages of the new approach, planners would have to settle for using information that was less than perfect. But by asking the right questions they would at least be nudging collectors of information in the right direction.

The alternative approach outlined in this paper has something in common with the 'new approach' to manpower planning discussed earlier, the advocates of which would like training systems to become largely self-regulating, with decisions about content and quantity in the hands of employers, and planners playing only a facilitating role. However, whatever the progress towards this goal (and it is likely to be slower than some of its advocates hope) the need to look forward to future directions for some types of training will remain. For this purpose some combination of current rate of return analysis and analysis of expected structural change in the economy, such as that proposed in this paper, will be needed.

References

Ahamad, B. and M. Blaug, 1973. *The Practice of Manpower Forecasting: A Collection of Case Studies*, Elsevier, Amsterdam.

Amjad, Rashid, 1985. ARTEP's Experience in Short and Medium Term Employment Planning (mimeo.), ILO-ARTEP, New Delhi.

Amjad, Rashid, 1987. *Human Resource Planning: The Asian Experience*, ILO-ARTEP, New Delhi.

Arcelo, Adriano A. and Bikas C. Sanyal, 1987. *Employment and Career Opportunities after Graduation: The Philippine Experience*, International Institute for Educational Planning/ Fund for Assistance to Private Education, Manila.

Clark, David H., 1986. 'Manpower Planning: Its Contribution to Vocational Training Planning', in Indonesian Manpower Management Information System.

Cohen, S.I., 1986. 'Labour Analysis and Manpower Planning: Examples from Comprehensive Technical Cooperation Programmes on Human Resources', in Indonesian Manpower Management Information System.

Dore, R.P., J. Humphrey and P. West, 1976. 'The Basic Arithmetic of Youth Employment: Estimates of School Outputs and Modern Sector Vacancies for Twenty-five Countries', 1973 and 1980, *World Employment Programme Working Paper* (WEP 2-18/WP 9), ILO, Geneva.

Dougherty, Christopher, 1983. 'Manpower Development from Three Points of View: Country, Technical Assistance Agency, and Lending Agency', Ch. II in Psacharopoulos *et al.*

Dougherty, Christopher, 1986. 'Technological Change and Manpower Development Planning', in Indonesian Manpower Management Information System.

Godfrey, Martin, 1991. *Education, Training and Employment: What can Planners Do?*, ILO-ARTEP, New Delhi.

Hasibuan, Sayuti, 1986. 'A New Approach to Manpower Planning', in Indonesian Manpower Management Information System.

Hollister, Robinson, 1967. *Technical Evaluation of the First Stage of the Mediterranean Regional Project*, OECD, Paris.

Hollister, Robinson, 1983. 'A Perspective on the Role of Manpower Analysis and Planning in Developing Countries', Ch. III in Psacharopoulos *et al.*

Hollister, Robinson, 1986. 'Manpower Planning Viewed as an Analysis Process for Manpower and Employment Policy Formation and Monitoring', in Indonesian Manpower Management Information System.

Hunting, Gordon, Manuel Zymelman and Martin Godfrey, 1986. *Evaluating Vocational Training Programmes: A Practical Guide*, World Bank, Washington.

Indonesian Manpower Management Information System, 1986. *Report on the Seminar: New Orientations of Manpower Planning and Analysis and Their Relevance to Indonesia*, ILO/UNDP Project INS/85/034, Jakarta.

Jolly, Richard and Christopher Colclough, 1972. 'African Manpower Plans: an Evaluation', *International Labour Review*, 106: 2–3, August–September.

Mehmet, Ozay and Yip Yat Hoong, 1986. 'Human Capital Formation in Malaysian Universities: A Socio-Economic Profile of the 1983 Graduates',

Occasional Papers and Reports, No. 2, Institute of Advanced Studies, University of Malaya, Kuala Lumpur.

Psacharopoulos, George and Keith Hinchliffe, 1983. 'From Planning Techniques to Planning Process', Ch. I in Psacharopoulos *et al.*

Psacharopoulos, George and Maureen Woodhall, 1985. *Education for Development: Analysis of Investment Choices*, Oxford University Press, New York.

Psacharopoulos, George, Keith Hinchliffe, Christopher Dougherty and Robinson Hollister, 1983. 'Manpower Issues in Educational Investment: A Consideration of Planning Processes and Techniques', *World Bank Staff Working Papers*, Number 624, World Bank, Washington.

Sanyal, B.C., L. Yaici and I. Mallasi, 1987. *From College to Work: The Case of the Sudan*, International Institute of Educational Planning, Paris.

Statistics Canada, 1989. *Follow-up of 1982 Graduates: Survey Methodology Report and User's Guide*, Ottawa.

Youdi, R.V. and K. Hinchliffe (eds), 1985. *Forecasting Skilled-Manpower Needs: The Experience of Eleven Countries*, International Institute of Educational Planning, Paris.

Discussion

A review of the paper was made by Dr Rabindra Kumar Shakya of the National Planning Commission Secretariat, Government of Nepal. He noted that the Manpower Requirements Approach (MRA) has been widely criticised because it cannot derive an economy's training needs correctly, and yet a majority of the Asian countries use this approach. However, the alternative approach is not any easier to use; forecast of structural change is difficult, and so is rate-of-return analysis. However crude the MRA may be, it does supply certain information to planners, such as the trends in an economy, and it is therefore not so surprising that decision-makers still opt for it.

The reviewer pointed out that whichever approach one chooses, it is timely and relevant statistics that are needed in most Asian countries. The availability of such data varies greatly from one country to another. In Nepal, a Labour Market Information System is yet to be established. The lack of data has left many countries adrift in terms of training plans. The information required for manpower planning is not always available and the planners' work is dictated by the availability of information and resources. Despite this, the MRA is still useful for forecasts both in the public and private sectors.

A participant from the Philippines commented that planning is necessary for certain occupations such as teaching and medicine. He also voiced the opinion that manpower projections have to take structural adjustment into consideration.

A participant from Malaysia commented that the limitations of the MRA are well documented. Citing an example of the MRA causing malfunctions in Malaysia, he related how over-production of engineers had taken place in the face of a recession. He supported the alternative approach, since it would satisfy those who believe in forecasting and at the same time help the planner to better understand the labour market.

A Chinese participant argued that one approach need not exclude the other; since no absolute solution can be found to labour shortages and labour surpluses, different approaches should be applied.

A participant from Thailand explained how projections based on inadequate data could lead to difficulties in decision-making. Improvement in data collection would be required to make manpower planning useful.

A participant from the ILO, Geneva, raised the point that many a plan has been evolved that nobody knows what to do with. Therefore, one has to ask, "what information do we need, and why", before starting any survey or planning process. At the same time, the planner must realise that the questions that can be answered are limited. The ILO participant also agreed that structural change, which is taking place in many Asian countries, has to be taken into account, and its impact on labour markets and skills training needs to be understood. The need for skills upgrading is becoming more apparent as economies open up and new technologies appear.

A Sri Lankan participant said that in his country, a simulation model based on capital output ratios is used, and opinion surveys are carried out amongst employers. A vocational training authority with representatives from the government, employers and employees has been established.

A Pakistani participant argued that for the purpose of drawing up five-year plans, the MRA cannot be totally dispensed with. This would in particular apply to training programmes with long lead-times. An Indian participant, on the other hand, stressed that the MRA at best can be used as an indicator, but it is not really of any help to those who have to make decisions about training. In India, the Directorate of Employment and Training has decentralised these decisions to the training institutions. Employers are requested to approach the institutions with specific requests according to which training programmes are tailormade.

A participant from Bangladesh related how bureaucratic and political decisions influence choices in the educational sector, rather than economic or rate-of-return criteria. He also argued that the social rate of return is very important, but difficult to calculate.

An Indonesian participant suggested that the MRA should be used for macro-level planning and demographic planning, while a micro-level approach could be used in industries and firms. He also commented that there is a problem of bias in the calculation of rate-of-return, since wages do not always reflect the quality of manpower.

Finally, the representatives from Mongolia described the problems that their country is undergoing in the transition from a centrally planned system to a market economy. Unemployment has risen from 0 in 1988 to 10 per cent currently, and is expected to continue rising. The entire population of 2 million is literate, but half of it is under 16 years of age. Training needs are great, but difficult to assess due to the total absence of data bases and information. Thus, training decisions cannot be made and the training system is going through a crisis.

Responding to the comment that disagreed with the opinion quoted in the paper that skill shortages "are not of crucial concern", Dr Godfrey agreed that, this is indeed an excessively sweeping statement from a proponent of the 'new approach'. It applies only to economies with fairly well-functioning training systems. Regarding the discussant's view that the alternative approach also is not easy and rate-of-return estimates are problematic Dr Godfrey agreed that much judgement is needed in correcting for biases, but at least the method asks the right questions. In reply to the comment that there are occupations for which planning is necessary (e.g., doctors) he pointed out that the paper recognises that demographic/political norms can be used for some occupations (e.g., doctors, nurses, teachers, police). But labour market factors still have to be taken into account; if salaries are too low, training and/or recruitment targets will not be met. Agreeing with the Malaysian participant that the MRA can cause malfunctions (e.g., over-production of engineers in Malaysia), Dr Godfrey said that the example is a good one. In many countries manpower projections show a 'shortage' of engineers, whereas engineers' salaries (and the rate-of-return) are low. In response to the comment from China on the nature of academic disputes he stressed that the alternative approach is in this spirit, taking something from both the rate-of-return and the forecasting approaches. He agreed with the Thai participant that lack of information makes it difficult to influence policy. Hence the need to improve the quality of information through tracer studies. Agreeing to the comment that all planning should start with the question "why do we need this information?" Dr Godfrey expressed the view that there should be as little planning as needed, rather than as much as possible. Regarding the use of employers' opinion surveys in Sri Lanka, he found these to be in the spirit of the alternative approach and said that it would be useful to know more about them. To the comment from Pakistan that long lead-times in education and training mean that the MRA cannot be dispensed with, he replied that there certainly is a need to look forward, but one does not necessarily have to use the MRA to do so.

He welcomed the information from India that a decentralised approach to training, with employers' involvement, is already in operation and added that this is a useful model, from which others can learn. To the point raised by a Bangladeshi participant that rate-of-return is difficult to calculate for social projects and that rates can be 'manufactured', opening the way for bureaucratic/ad hoc influences on choice of projects, Dr Godfrey replied that calculation problems are not inseparable, and the method is open to abuse, as are other methods. Responding to the comment from Indonesia that the MRA can be used for macro/demographic planning and a micro-approach at the operational level, he said that projections can be used for the demographic norm occupations (though this is not the MRA), and the micro-approach for others, in line with what is suggested in the paper. Responding, finally, to the description from Mongolia of an economy and education/training system in crisis, Dr Godfrey said that a different approach is needed for managing the transition rather than to manage a functioning market economy.

4

Interventions in Rural Labour Markets: A Review of Some Asian Experiences

PIYASIRI WICKRAMASEKARA

Rural workers constitute the largest segment of the work force in Asian developing countries. Despite increasing attention in recent literature to the issue of hired labour, the knowledge base with respect to factors governing their livelihoods can hardly be considered satisfactory.[1] Recent studies have mostly focussed on the impact of new technologies and working conditions. The objective of this paper is to focus on selected interventions for safeguarding the living conditions of rural workers. In section 4.1 some observations on the nature of the labour market in rural areas and its implications for intervention are outlined. This is followed by a discussion of selected interventions. The final section raises a number of issues for further discussion.

The present paper is based on several studies conducted by ARTEP on the conditions of rural workers and interventions. The term 'intervention' is used in a broad sense to include both policy interventions by the government as well as worker initiatives to improve their employment conditions.

4.1 Nature of Rural Labour Markets and Implications for Intervention

Rural workers basically comprise agricultural workers (in the smallholding and plantation sectors), the self-employed and others engaged in non-agricultural rural occupations. The informal nature of work contracts, predominance of casual workers, multiplicity of income sources and extra-market relations characterise the rural sector. In this sense, it differs markedly from the urban sector labour markets.[2]

---

1. In the case of India, the conditions of rural labour have been extensively documented. Several government-sponsored Rural Labour Enquiry Commissions have been set up over the years, with one Commission currently in session. These have gathered useful evidence on the condition of rural labour in different parts of the country.

2. K.P. Kannan (1990) has succinctly summarised the differences.

Rural employment differs from urban employment, especially industrial employment, in a number of respects. The identity of a person is not merely that of a worker in an impersonal work environment but is

Research carried out under the World Employment Programme indicate that rural labour markets are in a process of evolution and factors affecting returns to labour are too complex to be explained by markets alone. The concept of livelihood or survival strategies adopted by rural labour has been found to be crucial in understanding the outcomes of labour arrangements.[1]

A key factor to be considered here is the heterogeneity of the rural labour group.[2] Wage employment in rural areas is invariably linked with other forms of employment such as in small-holder farming, share-cropping and other non-farm economic activities. The multi-occupational structure of the typical labour household had been observed as a survival strategy in the face of uncertain and undependable incomes from only one source. In view of the close linkages between land, labour and credit markets, market relations alone cannot explain the processes of determination of wages and incomes of rural labour. The labourers may be part-time share-croppers or small farmers heavily dependent on landlords for credit and other requirements.

To quote from P.C. Joshi (1989):

> ...the appraisal of the problem of rural labour in India as in other Asian countries will remain only partial, limited and incomplete if we restrict our discussion to the landless labourers only and leave out of the scope of our discussion petty cultivators who are half-peasants and half-labourers only and whose very livelihood requires resort to sale of labour power for varying durations (p.22).

The implications of these characteristics of the rural labour market for policy intervention are several.

In terms of policy implications, this means that state interventions, if confined to the sphere of wage-employment alone (e.g. minimum wage legislation), are unlikely to produce the intended results; on the other hand, intervention in other spheres (e.g. credit relations) may improve conditions of wage labour (ILO, 1985).

Another implication is that it is difficult for rural labourers to organise autonomously. These organisations have come up mostly as a result of

---

(Footnote continued from page 86)

located in a social milieu which takes note of other important dimensions of this identity such as social status and gender. In addition an individual worker's relationship with the employer often transcends a one-to-one relationship but becomes a complex one in which the former's household as a whole may be dependent on the employer's household.... Furthermore, there may not be the advantage of numbers at the workplace as in the case of urban factory employment. In most cases labourers would be working in small groups (as in agriculture) or dispersed in household manufacturing. There is also the situation, as in Indian agriculture, of a large number of employers so that the rural labourers are not faced with a few employers against whom they can organise.

1. See Radwan (1989) for a summary of this work. Also see Amit Bhaduri (1989) and Krishna Bharadwaj (1989).

2. Bharadwaj for instance distinguishes between four types of groups in the rural sector and argues that the first two groups are compelled to engage in compulsive exchange relations. Moreover, there is a tendency on the part of small farmers to hang on to tiny holdings. It is argued that such behaviour leads to underformation of the rural labour market.

interventions from outside the rural milieu, as part of a wider social/political mobilisation.

Recent evidence points to some disturbing trends in regard to the landless rural wage workers in Asian countries, particularly India (V.S. Vyas, 1990). Low wages, lack of protection, and limited and uncertain work opportunities characterise the conditions of landless rural workers. The landless workers are generally more vulnerable since they have no assets whatsoever to tide over problems of seasonality or lack of work opportunities. Policies applied to the small-farmer sector are of no direct benefit to the rural landless. Another disturbing trend observed is the increasing casualisation of rural labour from permanent or regular categories. This has been observed in Pakistan and India in various locations (see Kalpana Bardhan, 1989; Irfan, 1989; Akmal Hussain, 1988). Recent structural adjustment programmes pursued by various countries have also adversely affected the landless labour households in several ways. The impact has been felt in the form of reduced real wage rates and incomes and decreases in state welfare benefits resulting from cuts in public expenditure (Frances Stewart, 1987). The worst affected are the unorganised casual workers in the rural sector.

Given that most of the poor depend on wages for their incomes, the trends in returns to labour are interesting. Except in some Asian countries, Shovan Ray (1987) finds that real wage rates have actually declined.

A report by a Parliamentary Sub-committee of India on unorganised labour stated in 1987:

> Agricultural workers constitute the most backward, unorganised, downtrodden sector of the work force. They are mostly below the poverty line and have really been deprived of the fruit of their own labour over decades and even today do not get an adequate share of the fruits of planned economic development.

4.2   Types of Intervention

Given that free operation of rural labour markets may not ensure the best outcomes in terms of wages and incomes for the rural labour group, what type of intervention are possible? How did we categorise these interventions?

The measures can first be classified as long-range and short-term measures. In the long-term, improving mobility through training and education of workers' families and asset transfer schemes would assume priority.[1] Short-term measures would consist of legislation governing wages and working conditions, collective

---

1. Kalpana Bardhan (1987) has drawn attention to this stratification of job access for landless rural labour families. This can be remedied "with a combination of policies involving asset distribution, targeted training and placement and transfer payment (or relief programmes like the public works)... one could add the need for a much stronger commitment to crash programmes for schooling of children of landless/semi-landless labour families, and for homestead entitlement of landless labourers. These two should be highly prized elements of asset distribution" (p. 77).

Land and agrarian reform in the sugar sector of the Philippines, particularly in Negros Occidental has been pointed out as a major step for improving the situation of displaced sugar workers (see FAO, 1987).

agreements, etc. A distinction may also be drawn between general policies and target-group oriented policies. One may also distinguish between state intervention and private sector intervention.

Two broad groups of interventions are adopted for the present discussion.

4.2.1 State Intervention

(*i*) Policies for improving the operation of rural labour markets and contracts; minimum wage legislation, regulation of work hours, etc.

(*ii*) Measures to guarantee increased wage-based employment through employment generation schemes.

The Employment Guarantee Scheme for Maharashtra state is the best known example of this type in India. Rural works programmes can be considered under this category since the basic objective is to provide wage employment to the landless rural workers in most instances. (Muqtada, 1990; Mazumdar, 1989; Bandhyopadhyay, 1987.)[1]

(*iii*) Intervention in the creation of non-wage based employment and income generation. Preferential access to credit and asset transfer have been proposed in this area for generation of incomes through self-employment for labour households. The IRDP in India is a case in point.

(*iv*) Improving resource position of workers through asset and land redistribution.

We shall focus on the first two types in this paper.

4.2.2 Rural Workers Organisations

The basic function of these organisations will be to exercise some bargaining power over wages and employment levels by controlling the supply of labour.[2]

Another factor which can influence both wage rates and employment opportunities is the phenomenon of labour migration, though it does not fall strictly within the above types of intervention. It would influence the supply of labour and thereby affect wage and employment opportunities across regions. This can take the form of temporary (circular) as well as permanent migration.

---

1. "Availability of employment in government sponsored public works helped to increase the general level of wages in the countryside. Wage rates being the most portent instrument of transfer of income to the poorest section, imaginative use of NREP can help significantly in boosting it." See Bandhyopadhyay (1986), p. 24.

2. "...access to income by the rural poor is governed by political as well as economic conditions. Accordingly the development of organisations through which the rural poor can articulate and protect their interests is an essential precondition for any sustained improvement in their position." See Gillian Hart (1984).

In the case of the Philippines, the potential of these organisations to resist the adoption of labour-saving technology and also gain land access from the landed class has been highlighted (Bautista, 1987).

"Encouraging the organisations of labour groups, and using their agency and active involvement in recruiting labour, designing projects, and administering the relief components can be very valuable for the cost-saving and the safeguarding roles, apart from generating training and feedback effects" (Kalpana Bardhan, 1989, p. 78).

Interstate disparities induce such labour flows within India on a large scale. In Pakistan the withdrawal of labour through out-migration from the rural sector to the Middle East is said to have pushed up rural wages. (ILO-ARTEP, 1987).

The paper draws on studies carried out in three countries in South and South East Asia (India, the Philippines and Pakistan), among others. The impact of rural workers organisations has been studied with particular reference to the sugar sector in the Philippines (Negros) and Kerala state in India. The Philippines study focusses on sugar workers in the Philippines who have been badly affected by the slump in the sugar industry, experiencing sharp declines in both real wages and employment among sugar workers. The Maharashtra study examines the effect of employment guarantee schemes on income and employment of rural labour. Pakistan shows the fortunes of rural labour in the absence of any major intervention by the state or organisation among workers.

4.3 Studies of Interventions

4.3.1 *State Intervention in Rural Labour Markets*

State intervention has taken two forms: direct intervention and indirect intervention. Direct interventions have aimed at producing an impact on the rural labour market, such as institutional changes to increase the existing wage rates and employment. Indirect interventions do not aim at a direct impact on the labour market, but to achieve certain social objectives which in turn effect changes in the status of rural labour.

In the case of Kerala, there has been extensive intervention both directly and indirectly (Kannan, 1990). Under direct intervention, security of homestead land which enhanced the organised bargaining power of rural labour and thereby resulted in an increase in the reserve price of labour is important. Next comes the setting of minimum wages. These levels are determined by tripartite committees consisting of representatives of government, workers and employers. Setting of minimum wages is based on the concept of a 'need-based wage for subsistence'. The main impact of this has been an increase in collective bargaining power and considerable reduction in the authority of employers. Industrial relations committees which mediate between unions and representatives of employers constitute another important measure. These have helped in reducing the tensions between workers and employers by bringing them together for negotiations.

Two other areas where the state has played a role are: promoting labour cooperatives and implementing rural employment programmes.

Indirect interventions comprise various consumption subsidising programmes such as PDS and other welfare schemes for the weaker sections. Kannan (1990) has estimated that the money equivalent of the consumption subsidy adds up to the per capita consumption of one member of the family. The most important of these is the system of public distribution of foodgrains (and other essential commodities), the gain from which is close to half the total consumption subsidy. Another welfare scheme is the pension to aged agricultural labourers. These schemes have increased the purchasing power as well as the bargaining power of rural labour.

The combined impact of all the state interventions has been to raise the reserve price of labour over a period of time. The interesting feature of the Kerala experience is that while no basic restructuring of the distribution of assets in favour of landless rural labourers took place, various forms of state intervention have helped the rural workers to gain a measure of economic security. This indicates that interventions even in limited areas which ease the extreme social and economic disadvantages of rural labourers can go a long way.

Gujarat has experimented with a number of innovative programmes for the weaker sections in the state. A major step is the establishment of Rural Workers' Welfare Centres for the rural poor. This programme has the objective of organising the rural poor in the state by undertaking various welfare and developmental activities.[1] It goes beyond the central scheme of appointing Honorary Rural Organisers in all the states. Multiple activities are undertaken by the RWWC. Hirway and Abraham (1990) found that while the scheme has many positive points, it also demonstrates the limitations of government action:

> ...the activities of the centres have not been able to provide much support to rural workers in terms of providing them protection from the various types of exploitation of these workers. It appears that the government does not even encourage their activities as these are likely to cause conflicts in rural areas. For example, the contribution of the scheme in the implementation of minimum wages has been negligible (p. 98).

Minimum wage legislation. We shall now look at minimum wage legislation which is a common form of state intervention drawing largely on the Indian experience. Virtually all governments have accepted in principle the need for fixing minimum wages for rural labourers. The general objectives of minimum wage fixing are: to prevent exploitation, to give workers a reasonable standard of living, to eliminate unfair competition and to ensure more equitable growth and distribution of income (see ILO, 1975).

India has a long history of minimum wage legislation covering the rural sector. Minimum wages for agricultural labour was enacted as far back as 1948 by the Minimum Wages Act of 1948. Yet this act does not lay down the criteria for fixing minimum wages. State governments have to fix minimum wages in their respective states for labourers and revise them periodically if required. (See NIRD, 1989). The problem is that minimum wages have not been revised at fixed intervals. The Labour Ministers' Conference of 1980 proposed linking of agricultural wages to cost of living or revision of rates every two years, and some states have already adopted this proposal. Also, most state governments have no rational system for fixing minimum wages. In contrast, the West Bengal government has an elaborate scheme for this purpose.

In order to strengthen the enforcement machinery, Rural Labour Commissioners were appointed in Gujarat and Bihar. A pilot scheme for more intensive labour inspection in agriculture through appointment of Rural Labour Inspectors has been implemented in Madhya Pradesh, Manipur, Orissa and Rajasthan, as

---

1. See Hirway and Abraham (1990) for a detailed exposition and evaluation of this experiment.

part of a centrally sponsored scheme. Another important piece of legislation is the Interstate Migrant Workmen's Act which covers agricultural workers.

Recent studies have highlighted the wide variation in actual wage rates across states and the deviation from minimum wages. (Ministry of Labour, Government of India, 1990; NIRD, 1989; A.V. Jose, 1988). The Parliamentary Sub-committee Report (1987) found non-payment of minimum wages to be generally the case. The findings of the National Commission on Rural Labour on the basis of information obtained from state governments revealed the following. The daily wages paid ranged from Rs 8.50 in Andhra Pradesh to Rs 33.00 in Punjab. In most cases wages paid were less than minimum wages. The Commission attributes non-payment of minimum wages to the following factors: ignorance of existing labour laws; non-availability of regular employment, lack of organisation of rural workers, caste and social barriers, landholding patterns, inadequate enforcement machinery; vested interests of politicians and landlords; and indebtedness and bondage.

The Labour Ministers' Conference of 1987 recommended the following measures to make implementation of minimum wages more effective.

(*a*) A publicity campaign to create awareness about the act.
(*b*) Strengthen the enforcement machinery of state governments.
(*c*) Improve mobility and security of inspection staff.

Breman (1983) and Hirway and Abraham (1990) have shown the difficulties in implementing minimum wage laws in the specific case of Gujarat. The later study reported that Voluntary Rural Organisers who were expected to help in the enforcement of the Minimum Wages Act found it a task beyond their capacity.

There has been some debate on fixation of a national minimum wage and regional minimum wages. The 36th session of the Labour Ministers' Conference in 1987 addressed this issue. The sub-committee tried to lay down guidelines for minimum wages. It felt that consumption needs, poverty line, etc. should be taken into account in the fixation of minimum wages.

International experience in the implementation of minimum wage laws in the rural sector is not encouraging. Generally these are said to be more effective in the case of plantation or estate workers (ILO, 1988a, 1988b). Given the characteristics of rural labour, implementation of minimum wage laws is extremely difficult and the administrative machinery in most countries is simply not equal to the task.

> The seasonal character of employment, the wide scatter of places of employment, uncertain (and in some cases, near-feudal) work relationships, the use of payments-in-kind, widespread underemployment, and the often desperate poverty of the workers—all these make it very hard to implement the laws.

It is also argued that employment may suffer because employers may adopt labour-saving methods. The evidence from Kerala to be discussed later supports this to some extent.

Employment generation schemes. One major area of government intervention has been to create additional opportunities for wage-based employment or self-employment through public works or other programmes. This is expected to compensate for the high level of under-employment in rural areas. They offer short-term employment and also create physical infrastructure. Self-employment schemes take on a number of forms in different countries but essentially comprise asset endowment, skill development and entrepreneurship training programmes (Muqtada, 1989).[1] We shall focus only on wage employment schemes which are directly oriented to the target group of landless rural labour (Wickramasekara, 1990).

India has a long history of such schemes, dating back to the early 1960s. The major ones are: the National Rural Employment Programme (NREP), the Rural Landless Employment Guarantee Programme (RLEGP) and the Maharashtra Employment Guarantee Scheme (MEGS).[2]

The NREP was launched in 1980. It is included in the five-year plan and is implemented as a centrally-sponsored scheme with equal cost-sharing by the centre and the states. The programme has three objectives: generation of additional employment to the rural poor, creation of productive community assets for benefit of poverty groups and improvement in the overall quality of life in the rural areas. It is implemented through District Rural Development Agencies (DRDAs) all over the country. Work is executed through Panchayat Raj institutions. Wages are paid partly in foodgrains. The programme has created about 3 billion mandays up to 1988.

Of particular interest from the viewpoint of the present paper is the RLEGP, launched in 1983. This was designed to reach the target group of hard-core poverty, particularly the landless. It guarantees employment to at least one member of every landless labour household up to 100 days in a year. While the scheme is fully funded by the Central Government, partial payment of wages in the form of grains is mandatory (Bandhyopadhyay, 1986). A total of Rs 6.5 billion was spent on the programme in 1987–88 and 303 million mandays were generated. The achievements have generally been in excess of the targets.

Though these two programmes have succeeded in reaching and even exceeding the physical and financial targets, various evaluation studies have revealed certain shortcomings (see Department of Rural Development, 1988). The programme coverage is uneven with a few pockets of concentration. The employment provided is also of short duration and does not have any real impact on the living conditions of rural labour. Leakages have been observed with the involvement of contractors and middlemen. There are also no proper arrangements for maintenance of assets created under the programmes.

The major focus of this paper is on the MEGS.[3] This scheme initially began as an ad hoc public works programme in the wake of a severe drought in the state of Maharashtra and was converted into a permanent programme in 1976. It is designed to provide unskilled manual work mainly during the slack season in agriculture. Work is guaranteed to all registered workers on demand and within close proximity. It is stipulated that at least 60 per cent of the total project expenditure should be on wages. The project work is undertaken by line

---

1. The IRDP (India), the Grameen Bank Scheme (Bangladesh), Youth Investment Promotion Society (Pakistan), NYSCO and Women's Bureau programmes (Sri Lanka), and KKK (Philippines) are examples.
2. The literature on these programmes are substantial. See Bandhyopadhyay (1986); Department of Rural Development, India (1988); Deolalikar (1987); Acharya (1990).
3. This section mainly draws upon Acharya (1990).

departments directly and not through contractors. The guarantee is for unskilled work and workers have no rights regarding the nature of work. The scheme is financed through the state budget and special taxes. A unique feature of the scheme is that it generates a large number of jobs yearly and is not restricted to a short period like other rural works programmes. In this regard, the EGS is perhaps the first programme which guarantees the right to work as a basic right in a developing country. The EGS has been devised with a view to providing a floor wage to workers on the one hand and continued employment, particularly during off-seasons, on the other hand.

The EGS, according to Planning Department figures, has been creating over half a million jobs per year throughout the 1980s. Since the mid-seventies the number of persons provided with jobs has almost doubled, though there has been no discernible trend (Table 1). Women form about 35–40 per cent of the total EGS workers (see Acharya, 1988). Since this corresponds to the participation rate of women in the labour force of the country as a whole, there seems to be no serious gender discrimination in EGS recruitment. The proportion of backward castes working on the EGS has gradually declined since the early eighties, which is a cause for some concern. As Acharya observes, the overall target group representation is, however, quite high (Table 2).

TABLE 1

Persondays of Employment Generated under the EGS annually in Rural Maharashtra

Year	Persondays ('000)
1975–76	1095
1976–77	1362
1977–78	1173
1978–79	1635
1979–80	2054
1980–81	1715
1981–82	1560
1982–83	1280
1983–84	1645
1984–85	1780
1985–86	1895
1986–87	1876

Source: Acharya (1990); Ministry of Planning, Government of Maharashtra

There are a number of evaluations of the scheme (see Deolalikar, 1987; Acharya, 1988; Deshpande, 1988). It is accepted that the MEGS has been able to reduce the extent of unemployment in general and female unemployment in particular and reduce fluctuations therein. The scheme has all along maintained a high labour intensity The ratio of expenses on wages (cash plus foodgrains) to total expenses has ranged between 68 and 75 per cent. The contribution to total rural employment has been estimated at 3 per cent and at about 8 per cent of total employment of the target group on the basis of 1983 data. The scheme has generated employment for between one-sixth to one-third of the rural unemployed and under-employed in the state since its inception. In Table 3, the share of EGS workers to total workers in rural Maharashtra (cultivators plus agricultural labourers) is shown in column 2. The Table shows that the share of EGS workers was 3.6 per cent for Maharashtra as a whole in that year. This indicates that in the absence of EGS, at least theoretically, unemployment would have been up by 3.6 per cent. Acharya notes that the proportion of EGS workers to agricultural labourers at 8.5 per cent or about one-twelfth of the total agricultural labourers implies that this is an impressive intervention per se. Critics argue that the extent of unemployment reduction is small and marginal. It is contested that such statistical calculations are based on

TABLE 2

**Year-Wise percentage of Females' and Backward Castes'
Attendance as on 31 March of the year from 1978–79 Onwards**

Year	Percentage of Female Labour Attendance	Percentage of Backward Class Labour Attendance
1978–79	43.3	41.9
1979–80	41.0	47.8
1980–81	37.3	44.5
1981–82	37.1	44.2
1982–83	36.9	35.6
1983–84	39.3	36.2
1984–85	37.9	34.7
1985–86	42.1	33.5
1986–87	52.9	—

Note : — data not available.
Source: Acharya (1990); Ministry of Planning, Government of Maharashtra.

TABLE 3

**Proportion of Agricultural Labourers and EGS Workers to the
Labour Force in 1981 by Region in Rural Maharashtra**

(Percentages)

Region	EGS Workers as a proportion of Agricultural Workers	Agricultural Labour as a proportion of Agricultural Workers	EGS Workers as a proportion of Agricultural Labourers
Konkan	1.63	20.88	7.81
South Maharashtra	3.52	31.96	10.99
Khandesh	5.24	47.36	11.01
Marathwada	3.68	44.26	8.32
Vidharba	3.32	60.69	5.47
Eastern Region	3.60	38.11	9.45
Maharashtra	3.59	42.30	8.48

Source: Acharya (1990); Calculated from *Census of India*, 1981 and Ministry of Planning, Government of Maharashtra Statistics.

inaccurate data. In view of these comments it could be argued that, while the EGS has contributed in easing underemployment in absolute terms, it has not affected the basic structure of the labour force. The reason is the very purpose for which the EGS was initiated, i.e. to provide jobs when all avenues are closed. Thus, the EGS especially provides employment to the category 'residual' workers who would be unemployed even during crop seasons.

More important is the impact on wages and incomes of labourers. It has been found that wage growth in real terms is insignificant (Acharya, 1990). This is partly due to the rule of maintaining the EGS wage at a level lower than the agricultural wage in the lowest agricultural wage zone, coupled with low agricultural growth experienced in the state during the eighties, official indifference or even malpractice. Wage rates have never been higher than subsistence level (Table 4).

TABLE 4

Real Wages (at 1970–71 prices) paid under the EGS and Prevalent in Agriculture, 1975–76 to 1985–86, in Rural Maharashtra

(Rupees per day)

Year	Real Wages under EGS (for both sexes)	Real Agricultural Wages	
		M	F
1975–76	1.59	1.79	1.29
1976–77	1.75	2.16	1.42
1977–78	1.95	2.32	1.57
1978–79	2.19	2.47	1.69
1979–80	2.30	2.27	1.52
1980–81	2.56	2.34	1.59
1981–82	2.63	2.26	1.51
1982–83	3.27	2.66	1.78
1983–84	3.20	2.79	1.84
1984–85	3.06	2.87	1.88
1985–86	3.39	3.75	n.a.
1986–87	2.77	n.a.	n.a.
Growth Rate	7.30	5.03	3.47

Source: Acharya (1990); Calculated by juxtaposing statistics from Ministry of Planning, Government of Maharashtra and Labour Bureau's Cost of Living Indices for Agricultural Labourers.

According to the ARTEP study, macro-statistics on poverty and micro-studies on incomes suggest that though the incomes of all may have risen, only those who initially earned enough to be near the poverty line may have crossed it. Those considerably below the poverty line reap only marginal benefits from the scheme. This is confirmed by Deshpande's findings as well. A detailed study of a taluka found that "the EGS provided a limited guarantee of employment.... Even with EGS participation, almost all the households sampled were below the poverty line" (Deshpande, 1988). It has also been noted that wages are at subsistence level and that there is a persistent wage gap between the earning of males and females.

In regard to asset creation, between 1975 and 1986, the number of projects sanctioned was 173, 244, out of which 64.3 per cent were completed. The ARTEP study notes the lack of coordination between the different maintenance agencies on the one hand and between the users and maintenance agencies on the other. It can be said that the position of the upkeep and utilisation of assets has not been uniformly satisfactory in all districts. "Though there is no direct evidence available on employment impact of the assets created except in the Ralegaon Shinde Village (study referred to elsewhere in this paper), the condition of the assets indicated that this would be minimal, if at all" (Acharya, 1990).

As far as Kerala is concerned, Kannan argues that state intervention in the area of rural employment generation is quite limited in contrast to welfare-oriented state intervention. Such rural employment programmes as are implemented arising out of the programmes sponsored by the Central Government are too meagre to make any perceptible impact on the economic condition of rural labourers. This highlights the need, or even urgency, for formulating rural employment programmes in the state.

Food for works programme: Philippines. The basic objective of the WFP/ILO Food for Work project was to generate employment opportunities to displaced sugar workers in the face of the crisis facing the sugar industry in Negros island. Bureaucratic delays hampered the programme from the inception in identifying suitable projects for assistance. Later, an informal network of NGOs collaborated with sugar planters to implement voluntary land-sharing schemes for which assistance was provided. Yet the most needy groups of agricultural labour who were on abandoned estates could not gain access to the scheme since landowners' consent was needed for such assistance (see Lopez-Gonzaga, 1988 and Mangahas, 1987). Moreover, the bulk of the projects supported belonged to agriculture and food production in contrast to the envisaged infrastructure development. Voluntary land transfer schemes arranged by NGOs yielded only temporary benefits. In most cases, the NGOs were established by the planters themselves.

4.3.2 Workers' Organisations

Given the problems of enforcement of protection mechanisms devised by the state and collusive arrangements between the rural elite and the enforcement machinery, there is a clear role for organisations of rural labour. These organisations can exert pressure to obtain improvements in working conditions for their members. The adoption of the Rural Workers' Organisations Convention (No. 141) in 1975 by the International Labour Organisation is a recognition of this basic right to organise.

The objectives and activities of workers' organisations may be based at the national level or at the regional level or confined to a particular trade (ILO, 1990). In the present context, we shall focus on Kerala state which has a high rate of unionisation and sugar workers in the Philippines.

What are the criteria for evaluation of the effectiveness or otherwise of workers' organisations? Workers' organisations may intervene at various levels and so too the state. Effectiveness can be evaluated in terms of economic and non-economic gains. The popular indicators of economic gains are the wage rate and the levels of employment and incomes. Attainment of social dignity, elimination of bondage and mobility are among the non-economic gains.

The Seminar on Rural Labour organised by the National Rural Labour Commission (Government of India, 1990) recognised the obstacles in organisation of rural labour. It noted that 90 per cent of the labour force in India is unorganised. Of these, assetless agricultural labourers are stated to be the worst affected. "Being poor, illiterate, ignorant, seasonally employed and scattered over remote corners of the country, they are the most unorganised among all the unorganised workers" (p. 44).

Rural workers' organisations in Kerala state. Kannan has analysed the condition of Kerala state which has a good record of unionisation of rural labour. Kerala forms an interesting case because of the high proportion of both agricultural and non-agricultural labourers in the rural work-force compared to the all-India level (Table 5). The majority of labour households are landless although officially Kerala has a low percentage of landlessness compared to all of India. The reason for this could be the distribution of homestead land to labourers in 1971 which provided them some basic form of landownership.[1] It is also to be noted that per capita employment is lowest, and both unemployment and wage rates highest in Kerala. This is a paradoxical situation in itself. There exists a large difference in wage rates for male and female workers.

TABLE 5

Percentage Distribution of Rural Workers according to Main Occupations

Category	1961			1971			1981 (Kerala)			1981 (India)		
	P	*M*	*F*	*P*	*M*	*F*	*P*	*M*	*F*	*P*	*M*	*F*
Cultivation	23	26	17	20	25	5	15	19	6	50	55	37
Agricultural Labourers	19	15	29	34	28	54	33	27	48	30	24	50
Livestock, fishing and plantations	9	11	6	8	8	6	10	11	8	3	3	2
Household industry	9	5	18	4	3	8	4	3	8	3	3	4
Manufacturing other than Household industry	8	8	7	10	10	12	10	10	12	3	4	2
Construction	1	2	N	2	2	N	3	3	1	1	1	1
Trade and Commerce	5	6	1	7	9	1	9	11	3	3	3	1
Transportation storage and communication	2	3	N	3	4	1	4	5	1	1	1	N
Other services	23	25	21	21	11	11	11	10	14	5	5	3

Note: N denotes negligible.
Source: Kannan (1990).

First, unions have been instrumental in getting minimum wages paid to their workers, in resolving disputes,[2] in setting up labour cooperatives in helping workers realise the welfare measures instituted by the state.

---

1. Kannan's study highlights the need for the labour group to have some land as a base, even a homestead allotment to reduce exclusive dependence on the landlord class. The situation of sugar workers in the Philippines provides a sharp contrast where they do not have any access to land and have to depend on the 'benevolence' of particular landlords. This is why the so-called voluntary land transfer scheme got so much prominence with PVOs acting as mediators. Where the NFSW got workers to do their own cultivation, there was noticeable lack of recognition by authorities to extend support to the workers.

2. The state has favoured the unions in the above respect by banning police intervention and setting up industrial relations committees.

TABLE 6

Average Daily Wage Rates of Rural Workers in Selected Occupations in Kerala

Year	PFLW	RCUSW	TPW	CFW	PFLM	RCUSM	RCMM	RCCM	RPM	TTM
1963-64	1.31	1.73	1.62	1.40	2.51	2.53	4.51	4.59	2.28	2.87
1964-65	1.53	1.75	1.76	1.22	2.84	2.56	4.60	4.70	2.38	3.80
1965-66	1.85	2.03	1.85	1.56	3.20	3.00	5.01	5.03	2.50	NA
1966-67	2.04	2.32	2.11	1.54	3.71	3.18	5.56	5.65	2.86	NA
1967-68	2.48	2.32	2.23	1.69	4.46	3.55	6.27	6.06	2.24	5.17
1968-69	2.57	3.22	2.39	2.15	4.73	4.95	7.68	7.68	3.43	NA
1969-70	3.01	3.59	2.66	2.90	4.90	5.49	8.27	8.12	3.89	NA
1970-71	2.79	3.68	2.78	3.12	5.09	5.40	8.30	8.19	3.75	NA
1971-72	3.54	3.83	3.06	NA	5.43	5.39	8.47	8.37	4.05	NA
1972-73	NA	3.90	3.49	NA	5.78	5.78	9.38	9.10	4.55	NA
1973-74	4.45	4.31	3.69	3.79	6.67	6.26	9.98	9.87	4.81	NA
1974-75	5.38	5.07	5.43	NA	8.05	7.31	11.59	11.60	7.23	NA
1975-76	5.77	5.93	6.26	6.67	8.57	8.48	13.25	13.30	8.37	NA
1976-77	5.89	6.48	5.70	7.89	8.44	8.75	13.94	13.93	7.60	9.77
1977-78	6.06	7.00	7.09	7.87	8.67	9.38	14.88	14.81	7.94	15.93
1978-79	6.26	7.32	7.18	8.16	8.99	9.86	15.37	15.23	8.29	19.83
1979-80	6.68	8.09	7.47	7.82	9.58	10.72	16.76	16.66	9.37	20.17
1980-81	7.91	9.62	10.01	7.88	11.13	12.30	18.75	18.66	10.31	23.73
1981-82	8.83	11.40	11.18	NA	12.74	15.22	22.66	22.52	12.54	27.50

(Contd.)

TABLE 6 (*Contd.*)

Average Daily Wage Rates of Rural Workers in Selected Occupations in Kerala

Year	PFLW	RCUSW	TPW	CFW	PFLM	RCUSM	RCMM	RCCM	RPM	TTM
1982–83	9.55	13.53	11.71	NA	13.29	17.85	28.13	27.99	13.84	24.30
1983–84	11.02	14.81	13.81	NA	15.86	20.29	33.29	33.43	16.14	24.30
1984–85	11.89	16.37	15.18	NA	23.60	21.90	36.65	36.71	17.69	21.87
1985–86	15.10	–NA	–NA	NA	26.08	–NA	–NA	–NA	–NA	–NA
1986–87	16.34	–NA	–NA	NA	28.82	–NA	–NA	–NA	–NA	–NA

Notes:

PFLW	=	Paddy field labour (women).
RCUSW	=	Unskilled women in rural construction.
TPW	=	Women in tea plantations.
CFW	=	Women in cashew factories.
PFLM	=	Paddy field labour (men).
RCUSM	=	Unskilled men in rural construction.
RCMM	=	Masons in rural construction (men).
RCCM	=	Carpenters in rural construction (men).
RPM	=	Men in rubber plantation.
TTM	=	Men in toddy tapping.

Sources: Kannan (1990); Government of Kerala, *Statistics for Planning*, various issues.
For RPM, Raman (1986)
For TTM, Kannan (1988 : 163)

TABLE 7

Compound Growth Rates in Daily Money Wages in
Selected Occupations in Kerala

Period	PFLW	RCUSW	TPW	PFLM	RCUSM	RCMM	RCCM	RPM
I	11.60	10.03	8.27	9.13	10.04	8.61	8.21	8.06
II	9.45	11.80	10.64	11.10	11.19	11.44	11.44	9.27

Notes: Period I = 1963-64 to 1973-74 (For PFLW 1963-64 to 1971-72).
Period II = 1974-75 to 1984-85 (For PFLW and PFLM 1974-75 to 1986-87).
PFLW = Paddy field labourers (women).
RCUSW = Rural construction unskilled labourers (women).
TPW = Tea plantation labourers (women).
PLFM = Paddy field labourers (men).
RCUSM = Rural construction unskilled labourers (men).
RCMM = Rural construction masons (men).
RCCM = Rural construction carpenters (men).
RPM = Rubber plantation labourers (men).
Source: Kannan (1990), computed from data given in Table 6.

What is more important from our point of view is union intervention in the labour market and the labour process. Kannan argues that it has been a crucial factor in the ability of workers and unions to increase the money wage rates. Union control over supply of labour has prevented erosion of wage levels (Tables 6, 7 and 8). Several methods have been used by unions to get control over workers and to realise their objectives.

Restricting entry into the job market or inter-occupational mobility has segmented the rural workers in a caste-based occupational distribution as was prevalent earlier. Rationing of employment has been resorted to provide employment to all the members by rotation where labour is in surplus.

Kannan argues that the role of labour in the production process is crucial for effective control over labour supply. Two examples are cited: workers in rural construction, and loading and unloading workers in quarrying.

Workers in rural construction enjoy one of the highest wage rates. Contractors hire labourers on higher wages because they can easily increase their profitability by raising the tender estimates by a greater margin. There has been a reduction in public works and thus a corresponding reduction in employment. In other words, the efforts of unions to increase wages to offset low employment has led to a fall in employment. In the case of quarrying, as labour is in surplus, work is shared on the basis of rotation (number of workers supplied is more than the number of workers required and thus workers work on rotation). This has made them keep the wage rate as high as possible since the wages collected by unions are distributed among all the workers.

In order to illustrate the operation of these factors, Kannan has undertaken case studies of organisation by three types of labourers: agricultural labourers, cashew processing workers and toddy tappers.

TABLE 8

Index Numbers of Real Wage Rates of Rural Workers in Selected Occupations in Kerala

Year	PFLW	RCUSW	TPW	CFW	PFLM	RCUSM	RCMM	RCCM	RPM	TTM
1963–64	100	100	100	100	100	100	100	100	100	100
1964–65	98	85	91	73	95	85	86	86	88	111
1965–66	104	87	84	82	94	87	82	81	81	NA
1966–67	107	92	90	76	102	87	85	85	86	NA
1967–68	122	87	89	78	115	91	90	85	63	116
1968–69	111	105	83	87	107	111	96	95	85	NA
1969–70	126	114	90	113	107	119	100	97	93	NA
1970–71	110	110	89	115	105	110	95	92	85	NA
1971–72	142	116	99	NA	114	112	99	96	93	NA
1972–73	NA	113	108	NA	116	115	104	100	100	NA
1973–74	136	100	91	109	107	99	89	86	85	NA
1974–75	119	85	97	NA	93	83	74	73	92	NA
1975–76	133	104	117	144	103	101	89	88	111	116
1976–77	153	127	120	192	114	118	105	103	113	194
1977–78	161	141	153	196	121	129	115	113	122	237
1978–79	163	145	152	199	123	133	117	114	124	226
1979–80	164	150	148	179	123	136	119	117	132	242
1980–81	176	162	181	164	130	142	121	119	132	254
1981–82	178	174	183	NA	134	159	133	130	145	—

(Contd.)

TABLE 8 (*Contd.*)

Index Numbers of Real Wage Rates of Rural Workers in Selected Occupations in Kerala

Year	PFLW	RCUSW	TPW	CFW	PFLM	RCUSM	RCMM	RCCM	RPM	TTM
1982–83	169	181	168	NA	123	164	145	141	141	197
1983–84	159	162	162	NA	120	152	140	138	134	161
1984–85	169	176	175	NA	175	161	151	149	145	142
1985–86	213	NA	NA	NA	192	NA	NA	NA	NA	NA
1986–87	208	NA	NA	NA	191	NA	NA	NA	NA	NA

Notes:
PFLW   =   Paddy field labourers (women).
RCUSW =   Rural construction unskilled labourers (women).
TPW   =   Tea plantation labourers (women).
PLFM   =   Paddy field labourers (men).
RCUSM =   Rural construction unskilled labourers (men).
RCMM   =   Rural construction masons (men).
RCCM   =   Rural construction carpenters (men).
RPM   =   Rubber plantation labourers (men).

Source: Kannan (1990).

(a) Agricultural labourers. Through a study of Kuttanad and Palghat districts, the author has tried to show the relevance of historical perspective in the organisation of rural labour.

Union intervention initially gave importance to the removal of social indignities of agricultural labourers and later on, to improvement in working conditions. Union intervention took place under severe constraints of high agrarian density and slow rate of growth in agriculture. In Kuttanad, labour had to play an important role in the labour process due to unfavourable ecological conditions and the large size of fields. Unions got the working hours reduced to eight hours and further to six hours by including the time spent in commuting to and from the work-place in a day's work. State intervention in the form of a ban on police intervention favoured the unions which were trying to get an increase in wages and also the determine the size of workers for a given operation. Unions were helped in achieving their objectives by the labourers' crucial role in the labour process.

Palghat presents a different picture. Due to favourable ecological conditions and the small size of farms, tension between farmers and workers was less. The role of labour in the labour process, thus, was not very crucial. Hence, despite organisation, the gains of labourers in Palghat were less impressive. Also, importation of labour was successful in Palghat whereas it failed in Kuttanad. Only the harvest wages in Palghat are comparable to those of Kuttanad.

As far as economic gains are concerned, wages and employment gains may be considered. The most important gain is in respect of wages. This has been possible because of unions. On the employment front, it is noted that there has been a decline in employment in Kerala. The reason could be the increase in money wages as the number of agricultural labourers has not increased significantly since 1971. Also, labour-displacing technologies have not been introduced on any significant scale, especially in Kuttanad.

Benefits other than increase in wage rates were largely obtained as a result of state interventions which were induced by the organised power of agricultural labourers. No fundamental re-distribution of assets or income through land reforms has taken place. Increases in wages have helped workers in crossing or coming closer to crossing the poverty line in spite of a decline in per capita employment.

(b) Cashew processing workers. The cashew processing workers are predominantly women. This industry requires cheap unskilled labour and little fixed capital. Both union and state interventions in this industry have, largely, met with failures due to the nature of the industry and the type of labour. Not much has been achieved in wage rates while employment has fallen (Tables 9 and 10). It is argued that state intervention failed because the industry was shifted to nearby states. The setting up of a public sector corporation and a cooperative has also not helped much. Union intervention has largely failed as women constitute more than 90 per cent of the total labour force in this industry.

(c) Toddy tappers. Organisations of toddy tappers have been quite successful in transforming their initial work conditions. Toddy tapping is a caste-bound skilled rural occupation. Apart from wage increases, unions have been successful in getting non-wage benefits also. Both state and union interventions have been

TABLE 9

**Difference between minimum wage rates and actual wage rates
(as per ASI) of cashew workers (Rs/day)**

Year	Average minimum wage	Wage rate paid as per ASI	Real wage rate 63/64 = 100
1959–60	1.50	1.06 (71)	
1960–61	1.68	1.23 (73)	
1961–62	1.83	1.28 (70)	
1962–63	1.90	1.59 (83)	
1963–64	1.90	1.40 (74)	1.40
1964–65	2.10	1.22 (58)	1.03
1965–66	2.33	1.56 (68)	1.15
1966–67	2.48	1.54 (62)	1.06
1967–68	3.48	1.69 (49)	1.09
1968–69	3.71	2.15 (58)	1.21
1969–70	3.83	2.90 (76)	1.58
1970–71	3.96	3.12 (79)	1.62
1971–72	3.96	NA	NA
1972–73	4.18	NA	NA
1973–74	4.93	3.79 (77)	1.52
1974–75	6.34	NA	NA
1975–76	8.56	6.67 (78)	2.02
1976–77	NA	7.89	2.68
1977–78	7.98	7.87	2.74
1978–79	8.29	8.16 (98)	2.79
1979–80	NA	7.82	2.51
1980–81	12.69	7.88 (62)	2.30

Notes: Figures in brackets indicate the actual wage rae as a percentage of statutory minimum wage rate. Real wage rates are obtained by deflating the money wages with the ACPI. Though the dearness allowance for cashew workers is paid according to the CPI for industrial workers in Quilon, we have used ACPI as the deflator for comparing the real wage rates of female agricultural workers and also to reflect the rural character of the workers.

Source: Kannan (1990).

TABLE 10

**Per capita employment and earnings of cashew workers
and female agricultural labourers**

Year	No. of days worked		Annual Earnings (Rs.)	
	Cashew	PFLW	Cashew	PFLW
1964–65	240	142	292	217
1974–75	163	139	1,087[a]	748
1979–80	93	NA	727	929[b]
				(748)[c]
1983–84	76[d]	112	NA	1,234

Notes: a. Wage rate used here is that of 1975–76 since the data for 1974–75 is not available.
b. Employment as per 1974–75 figures.
c. Employment as per 1983–84 figures.
d. Per capita employment in the public sector corporation. It is unlikely that the figure for the private sector is higher because a number of factories were closed during this year.

Source: Kannan (1990).

successful in this occupation due to the nature of the production process and the critical role of labour. The success is also to the fact that this industry faced inelastic demand and could not be shifted to the low wage areas as was the case with the cashew processing industry.

The Kerala experience shows that while it is possible to organise rural workers, some level of political impetus or external inducement is needed for organising labour. State policy has also favoured their role. Experiments at cooperativisation have been successful but their success varies from industry to industry.

Segmentation of the labour market on lines of caste and/or sex has affected workers belonging to the lower castes and women workers. At the same time, wage increases have not kept pace with productivity trends in agriculture (Tables 11,12).

The author argues that the experience of Kerala in terms of both organisation of rural workers and forms of state intervention can work as a model for other states. But the nature and form of organisations and interventions will have to be different depending upon the nature of the problems of the labour and the area of the concerned region.

TABLE 11

Rates of growth rate of NDP in agriculture at constant prices and of real wage rates in agriculture for Indian States between 1970–71 and 1984–85 classified as high, medium low and very low/negative growth rates

Growth rate of NDP in agriculture	States	Growth rate in real wage rates
High growth (3% and above)	Maharashtra (4.21)	Medium (1.74)
	Punjab (3.97)	Negative (–0.01)
	Gujarat (3.83)	High (2.23)
	Rajasthan (3.51)	Low (1.96)
	Orissa (3.12)	Medium (2.18)
Medium growth (2 to 3%)	Haryana (2.87)	Very low (0.85)
	Uttar Pradesh (2.79)	Low (1.82)
	West Bengal (2.54)	Very low (0.40)
	Karnataka (2.48)	Low (1.14)
	Assam (2.44)	Low (1.43)
	Andhra Pradesh (2.13)	High (3.44)
Low growth (1 to 2%)	Himachal Pradesh (1.89)	Very low (0.71)
	Madhya Pradesh (1.47)	Medium (2.94)
	Bihar (1.03)	Medium (2.41)
Very low or Negative growth (below 1%)	Kerala (–0.05)	Medium (2.42)
	Tamil Nadu (–1.35)	Low (1.23)

Source: Data reclassified from Jose (1988); Kannan (1990).

TABLE 12

Growth rates in land productivity and real wages
(Kerala: 1962/63–85/86)

Item	Period I	Period II	1962/63–85/86
Growth rate (all crops)			
Land productivity	1.70	0.20	1.05*
Real wage rate	–0.26	2.43*	0.82**
Growth rate (paddy crop)			
Land productivity	1.00*	1.20*	1.10*
Real wage rate	–0.14	7.71*	3.02*
Growth rate (other crops)			
Land productivity	2.00*	0.30*	0.97*
Real wage rate	–0.29	–0.87	–0.53

Notes: * Significant at 1%.
          ** Significant at 10%.
Source: Kannan and Pushpangadan (1988), cited in Kannan (1990).

Acharya (1990) has looked at the role of workers' organisations and their interaction with the MEGS. One could argue that such organisations can influence the scheme in order to ensure benefits to their members. Yet Acharya's survey highlights two main issues relating to intervention. First; the nature of the EGS has not permitted organisations of workers on a large scale and in a coherent way. Nevertheless, constant pressure to raise wages have yielded some results. Second, most intervening organisations had taken up the issue of EGS along with other issues prevalent locally in their regions. Acharya concludes: "Thus, while most accept the EGS to be a development programme, little effort has been made to give it that shape. More often, they indulge in fighting irregularities in its implementation".

Philippines sugar workers and unionisation[1]. In contrast to the urban sector, rural workers' organisations have been confined to the plantation and corporate farm sector only. Ofreneo (1990) estimates that the total number of unionised workers in agriculture will be in the range of per cent of the total labour force in agriculture. This discussion focusses on the sugar workers of Negros Island (the 'sugar bowl' of the Philippines) who have been adversely affected by the crisis in the sugar industry caused by falling world demand and low prices.

The collapse of sugar prices exposed the basic weakness of the sugar industry in the Philippines. The main impact of the shock was borne by labourers on sugar plantations. While labour unions have existed in Negros since the 1930s, it was only in the 1960s and early 1970s that the trade union movement gained ground. The Philippines experience is interesting in that it contrasts the experiences of a militant and a more conservative trade union movement in addressing the problems of workers. It also highlights the limitations of union action when the sugar plantation industry is in economic crisis.

---

1. This section draws heavily upon the study by Lopez Gonzaga (1988).

Today the leading labour unions are the National Federation of Sugar Workers (NFSW) and the National Congress of Unions in the Sugar Industry of the Philippines (NACUSIP). These two federations which command a broad influence in the national and international labour movement together comprised the vast majority of the organised and unionised workers in Negros. The NFSW focusses its efforts on the sugarcane workers while the NACUSIP serves both mill and farm workers.

NACUSIP is a trade union in the traditional mould which has emerged as the biggest labour federation in the entire sugar industry. It came about after the merger of two regional labour groups: the Confederation of Unions in the Sugar Industry (CUSI) in Luzon and the Council of Unions in the Sugar Centrals (CUSUC) in the Visayas. The majority of unions in the sugar mills are affiliated to NACUSIP.

NACUSIP started out and evolved as a traditional labour organisation primarily concerned with workers' bread-and-butter issues; its efforts mainly concentrated on improving the economic conditions of the workers through tactful diplomacy and negotiation rather than organisational strength and militant actions. The NACUSIP throughout the Marcos era was accused of being "pro-management". With the change in the political order, NACUSIP has gone through a process of reconsolidation and reassessment of its position.

Lopez-Gonzaga (1988) has compared and contrasted the performance of the two unions on several criteria: organisation, union benefits, programmes and implementation, orientation, organisational conduct. The overall conclusion is that the NACUSIP has been able to change its image somewhat and has also been more pragmatic in its approach with the end-result of yielding more benefits to members. While the NACUSIP has gained in membership, the NFSW is plagued by a gradual decline in its membership brought about lately by factionalism and the surging repression particularly by military elements and right-wing vigilante groups against the union. Also, the NFSW's far left position had alienated it somewhat from broad, popular support.

Table 13 summarises the main features of the two unions in a simplified manner.

Despite its largely conservative image during the previous regime, the NACUSIP's contributions to the development of the workers' cause in the sugar industry cannot be overlooked. It actively participated in 1968–69 in the establishment of the Social Amelioration Programme in the sugar industry and was instrumental in recently increasing the social amelioration bonuses of the sugar workers and the establishment of a death benefit programme for rural workers. In 1971, it initiated a review of and consequently an increase in the sugar workers' statutory minimum wages and in 1974, made a representation to the government to grant cost-of-living allowances (COLAs) to private sector workers. The NACUSIP succeeded also in standardising workers' benefits such as vacation and sick leave, retirement benefits and other fringe benefits not usually covered by legislations.

The advent of the sugar crisis exposed the limitations of their activities. Thousands of union members were suddenly out of work and even those who fortunate enough to hold on to jobs experienced very low wages and living conditions. Faced with such a grim situation, unions made representations with

TABLE 13
Features of the two major unions in Negros

Item	NACUSIP	NFSW
Scope	Workers' immediate issues	More political aims
Attitude	Conservative and now changing; generally pro-management; believes in tripartism	Militant; leftist and somewhat inflexible approach
Instruments	CBA, livelihood projects	CBA, livelihood projects; cooperative ventures
Other services	Worker education and training	Worker education and training
Present status	Re-assessment and reconsolidation in democratic context	Organisational and ideological controversies
State support	High during Marcos era; continued support with adaptation in present condition	Suppressed during previous regime. Initially supportive and later critical attitude to present regime.
Constraints	Initial credibility problem; resources; short-term outlook	Relative isolation due to militant position; resources

various government agencies and non-government organisations (NGOs) to launch immediate relief programme like emergency salary loans and rice loans to meet the workers' basic needs.

On behalf of its members, it also negotiated with sugar plantation owners the temporary use of vacant lands for food crop cultivation. Unions had to expand their existing socio-economic projects to accommodate urgent demands from displaced sugar workers. The NACUSIP spearheaded the National Tripartite Conference in the sugar industry in March 1988, resulting in the granting of a new wage increase to both industrial and agricultural sugar workers.

While both unions have taken quite a lot of effort in ensuring the economic upliftment of worker-members, through respective socio-economic programmes and livelihood projects the benefits that have accrued to the workers have been comparatively similar. In terms of wages and benefits, and job security, workers with collective bargaining agreements (CBAs) from both unions are better-off compared to those who have none. The SRC found that NACUSIP's CBAs are slightly better than that of the NFSW. Historically, the NFSW is relatively weak in negotiations with management due to its well-known militant attitude.

The NFSW and NACUSIP have made their socio-economic programme the centre piece of union work, especially in the wake of the crisis in the sugar

industry. Again, in scope and direction, the respective programme of both federations are more or less similar. Both federations engage to a great extent in landsharing
projects; the NFSW has its cooperative farm-lots while the NACUSIP opts for
workers' resettlement areas. Both have undertaken livelihood projects like cooperative stores, animal husbandry and livestock raising, food production, etc. Other
focal points of union assistance include trade union education and vocational
training and socio-cultural programmes.

As to the implementation of programme and projects, both unions have
experienced relative successes and failures. Generally the project beneficiaries of
both unions say that the programmes have been helpful in providing a better life
for them and their families. There is a consensus also that through the unions'
assistance they have been able to acquire higher wages and benefits, become more
aware of their rights and aspirations and avail of socio-economic programmes.
Over-all, most of the major socio-economic programmes and projects are implemented only as short-term or temporary measures and thus, are dependent on a lot
of variables.

Given the problems of sugar workers, much is still to be done. While the socio-
economic projects have provided some respite, there is still a long way to go. The
crisis in the sugar industry has seriously undermined the gains for members
(Ofreneo, 1990). Future prospects for the sugar industry leave no room for
complacency regarding dependence on wage employment alone for a livelihood.
In this context the passage of the Comprehensive Agrarian Reform Law (CARL)
has provided opportunities to the unions to undertake more broad-ranging
programmes (Ofreneo, 1990). Unions, particularly the NACUSIP have taken more
flexible, even improvised, approaches and positions. The NACUSIP has already
negotiated with the country's banking and finance institutions for the acquisition
and development, through lease-purchase agreements, of foreclosed lands for
workers' resettlement.

The Pakistan experience clearly shows that temporary gains by workers through
market forces may be short-lived in the absence of positive intervention by workers
or the state. Casualisation, job displacement and tenant eviction has occurred on a
mass scale in Pakistan (Hussain, 1990; Irfan, 1990). The real wage increases following
the massive exodus from rural areas to the Middle East along with the Gulf boom
were not maintained, as Irfan has shown. With return migration on a large scale,
the breakdown of traditional hiring arrangements and aggressive mechanisation,
workers find themselves in a worse position today.

4.4 Selected Issues

4.4.1 *Successful Experiences and Replicability*

The above review indicates that the claimed 'success' of certain models (workers'
organisations in Kerala, the EGS of Maharashtra) on closer inspection seem to be
qualified successes only. In the case of Kerala, the achievements are a qualified
success as Kannan shows that women and low-caste groups have been passed by
in the main benefits: "...the beneficiaries of much of the success of union intervention have been confined to men workers excluding those from the lowest castes.'
The EGS has had limited success as a poverty alleviation strategy, as shown earlier.

Moreover, success is related in some ways to specific factors. Kerala had a number of factors conducive to the successful working of unions. Some types of state intervention which have played an important role in the Kerala context seem to be absent in the all-India context. A sympathetic government was in place in Kerala, in contrast to the situation in a state like Bihar for instance, where organised violence against the weaker classes is common.[1] According to Kannan, a major factor is the distribution of small plots of land—homestead lands—to rural labour thereby snapping the grip of the landowners. Secondly, the role of the coercive apparatus of the state as embodied in the police policy has been such that its intervention has been restricted to issues other than labour disputes. The other elements of state intervention, namely those relating to direct and indirect consumption, are also equally important. "Such target-oriented schemes should provide a model to other states in India because of their redistributive impact—albeit limited—in the context of extreme inequality in wealth and income and the condition of severe poverty among the rural poor."

Workers' cooperatives have had mixed success as a replicable model in the case of Kerala. A success story is that of the beedi workers' cooperative in Cannanore district (Kannan, 1990). But in several other cases, labour cooperatives have failed to provide a credible alternative or preserve employment for the workers. The reasons for this have been traced to bureaucratisation of cooperatives, mismanagement and short-term political vested interests, in addition to structural constraints such as raw material shortage and competition. Howevever, workers' organisations have also failed in terms of their inability to counter the organisational shortcomings in these cooperatives.

In regard to the Employment Guarantee Scheme of Maharashtra, the most important element is the concept of guaranteed employment. It is important to recognise the concept of employment guarantee of the EGS has found wide acceptance in many areas such as the RLEGS and the Jawahar Rojgar Yojana (JRY).

Acharya has pointed out that the EGS has a lot of lessons to offer in terms of experience. First, an employment guarantee programme will have to generate enough employment for both the underemployed and the unemployed. In this regard, an important consideration is the provision of employment on a continued basis for a relatively long period, of say, 3-4 months. Yet this implies a major resource commitment on the part of the state.

He also suggests that the work should be spatially so distributed that mass migration of workers is kept at a minimum. This has generally been accepted in principle. The types of work and timings for initiation/closure should closely match the demands of village labour. Local public committees should be formed to help the administration draw up blueprints. Workers' representations could also find a place in these committees. It is also argued that the work under an employment programme should form a part of the total developmental plan of an area.

As far as wages are concerned, it is suggested that the wages should be reasonably high to help relieve workers of their poverty burden.

---

1. The same is true of Negros Island in the Philippines where vigilance groups have been mobilised by planters to forestall workers' attempts to gain land. Absentee landlords have organised themselves in preventing NFSW workers from harvesting crops.

The successful implementation of such a programme would require a balancing of several roles simultaneously. This could be achieved through planning for a cluster of villages and then successively coordinating at the block, district and state levels. The main constraint on this will be the absence of inter-departmental communication, which has always affected the EGS.

He concludes that EGS-type schemes can be replicated and improved upon, to supplement other poverty alleviation programmes. "Such an effort would, however, need more careful planning than that followed in the EGS in Maharashtra, specially in funds distribution, implementation of work and their usage, inter-departmental coordination, wage fixation and targeting."

4.4.2   *Complementarity of Programmes*

The analysis also highlights the complementarity of various programmes and interventions. Minimum wage legislation has been more successful in areas where workers' organisations have been strong. The EGS works have contributed more directly to worker needs where unions have been fighting irregularities in the system. It is also clear that public works projects should, as far as possible, provide examples to employers by adherence to minimum wage policies. Several studies show that resort to contractors for execution has quite often deprived workers of access to minimum wages.

Kannan shows the need in Kerala to supplement workers' organisation activities with government employment programmes.

> ...in the Indian context, organisation of rural workers is only a necessary condition but not a sufficient one to improve their livelihood. Inadequate employment opportunities is the crucial problem here. State intervention here could take the form of devising development strategies aimed at increasing labour absorption in agriculture especially through the provision of the two most important critical inputs—water and land development—as well as by initiating programmes for rural industrialisation. At the same time it has to be recognised that special employment programmes are also necessary to tackle the problem or rural unemployment especially targeted to the poorer sections... In sum, the tasks of creating the conditions for the organisation of rural workers and generation of employment in rural areas should be viewed as complementary tasks if the problem of rural poverty is to be eliminated within the foreseeable future.

4.4.3   *Trade-off between Employment and Wages*

An important issue to be considered is the trade-off between employment and wages. The Kerala experience shows a situation of rising wages and declining per capita employment. In some cases, this decline has been due to shift of industry and in some, due to higher levels of mechanisation.

Only toddy tappers were able to secure higher wages without suffering loss in employment and Kannan attributes this to the criticality of labour in the production process and the controlled entry into the industry due to caste orientation.

Another researcher has found this relationship in a different case study:

...there is an inverse relationship between the wage rate and the average number of days of work. The effect of this today is that for many of the formerly very militant agricultural labourers, the issue of permanency of employment has come to supersede the question of wage levels...landowners are constantly searching for ways to become less dependent on labourers, on introducing machinery to cultivating less labour-intensive crops. (Joan P. Mencher, 1988).

It is also stated that "Collective bargaining not only brought up their wages but also reduced their hours of work".

The issue to be raised is whether the relationship is this simple. Do unions gain much by fighting for higher wages if it leads to lower levels of employment? It has been maintained by Kannan that wages have been out of line with trends in agricultural productivity in Kerala. The issue, however, is whether the observed decline in employment can be traced to the trend in money wages only. It is known that Kerala has been characterised by industrial stagnation, which may account for the slow growth in employment. In the Philippines, sugar workers have to think of alternative avenues, given the general bleak prospects for the sugar industry.

4.4.4 Support for Rural Workers' Organisations

Given that spontaneous growth of unions or organisations of rural labour is not common, the issue of how to mobilise them for improvement of their working conditions is highly relevant. Should it be the role of the state? While the state can provide some assistance, it is not at all clear that it can become a driving force. Breman shows problems of state action in this respect in relation to the Bardoli district of Gujarat (Breman, 1987). The central scheme of appointing Honorary Rural Organisers at the block level is a positive step in this direction. Hirway and Abraham (1990) have documented the experience in Gujarat and concluded that limited success has been achieved in organising rural workers. In Kerala, the combined impact of the national political movement and state patronage was important. In some cases, NGOs can provide support.[1] Still, factors such as caste and creed act as driving forces in workers' organisations. (Breman, 1983; Kannan, 1990). Hence it is not possible to generalise on this issue. Given the numbers involved and the limited level of organisation achieved, there is scope for much more work for all agencies in this area.

4.4.5 Migrant Workers

The role and fortunes of migrant workers also merit further attention. Although some government legislation is available for their protection, they are among the most exploited in many cases. The use of migrant labour as strike-breakers is a common strategy (Breman, 1983). "For rural employers the migrants form an easily exploited category. They have to be content with exceptionally low wages and long, irregular working hours, easy to employ at short notice and at the same

---

1. See presentations by various NGOs about their activities in the National Rural Labour Seminar Proceedings.

time immediately replaceable." The relations between migrants and local landless labourers have, generally, been strained in such cases.

Some important issues in this respect are the following. What role can workers' organisations play? What can the government do to arrest migration flows? How can the government effect employment programmes in their villages of origin?

4.4.6 Wage Fixation Criteria; Minimum Wage Legislation and Public Works Programmes

Fixation of minimum wages has been a controversial issue all along. In general, the minimum needs criterion linked to the cost of living index and the need for periodic revision have been recognised. Another issue is the extent to which minimum wages should be adhered to in rural work programmes sponsored by this government. It has been argued:

> ...there is a strong case for integrating social legislation programmes like implementation of minimum wages with employment-based rural development programmes like the NREP. A strong case exists for instance for working out a uniform set of guidelines for the fixation of minimum wages and adequate weightage given to the minimum needs criterion and supplementing this with guaranteed employment at such wages for all willing workers in public works type rural development programmes. It is only by such interfacing of wage and employment guarantees that one can hope to make an effective impact on labour-market conditions in rural areas of the country. (Mukhopadhyay, 1987)

Acharya maintains that the wage should also be high enough to stabilise the agricultural wage in a region and should be based on the levels of living, the probability of a worker to obtain an incremental income which permits him/her to cross the poverty line, a halt in rural to urban migration, and permitting the programme to become self-targeting. While this is acceptable in principle, fixing a wage conforming to these criteria in practice will remain a formidable problem.

4.5 Concluding Observations

This paper has presented some experiences of state and union interventions based largely on the Indian experience. The complementarity of state and other interventions has been highlighted. In a long-run perspective, however, these interventions will have to be accompanied by more comprehensive structural reforms in rural areas (land reform, rural industrialisation, etc.) to meet the challenges of rural poverty and unemployment.

References

Acharya, Sarthi, 1988. *The Maharashtra Employment Guarantee Scheme; Impacts on Male and Female Labour*, The Population Council, Regional Office for South and South East Asia, Bangkok, March.

Acharya, Sarthi, 1990. *The Maharashtra Employment Guarantee Scheme; A Study of Labour Market Intervention*, ARTEP Working Papers, ILO-ARTEP, New Delhi, May.

ADB/ILO, 1987. *Rural Employment Creation in Asia and the Pacific*, Papers and proceedings of the ADB/ILO Regional Workshop on Rural Employment Creation, Asian Development Bank, Manila.

Bandhyopadhyay, D., 1986. *A Study on Poverty Alleviation in Rural India through Special Employment Creation Programmes*, ILO-ARTEP Working Paper, New Delhi.

Bardhan, Kalpana, 1983. *Economic Growth, Poverty and Rural Labour Markets in India: A Survey of Research*, World Employment Programme Research, Rural Employment Policy Research Programme, WEP 10-6/WP64, March.

Bardhan, Kalpana, 1989. 'Poverty, Growth and Rural Labour Markets in *India'*, *Economic and Political Weekly*, 25 March, pp. a-21–a-38.

Bautista, G.M., 1987. *The Impact of Agricultural Changes on the Rural Labour Market in the Philippines*, ARTEP Working Paper, March.

Bhaduri, Amit, 1989. 'Employment and livelihood. The rural labour process and transformation of development policy', Special issue on Rural Labour Markets and Poverty in Developing Countries, *International Labour Review*, Vol. 128 (6), pp. 685–704.

Bharadwaj, Krishna, 1989. 'The Formation of Rural Labour Markets: An Analysis with special reference to Asia', Rural Employment Policy Research Programme, WEP Research Working Paper, Geneva, May.

Breman, Jan, 1987. 'I am the Government Labour Officer...: State Protection for Rural Proletariat of South Gujarat', *Economic and Political Weekly*, Vol. XX (4), June 15, pp. 1043–1055.

Breman, Jan, 1985. *Of Peasants, Migrants and Paupers; Rural Labour Circulation and Capitalist Production in West India*, Oxford University Press, Delhi.

Damaso, Jimeno M., 1990. *Alternative Employment Creation Strategies for Plantation Workers in the Philippines*, a study prepared for the ILO ROAP and the TUCP, Philippines.

Deolalikar, A., 1987. 'Rural Employment Creation in India and Nepal', in ADB/ILO, *Rural Employment Creation in Asia and the Pacific*, Manila.

Department of Rural Development, 1988. *Report of the National Seminar on Poverty Alleviation Programmes*.

Deshpande, S.K., 1988. Local Level Management of a Rural Anti-Poverty Programme: A Case Study of the Employment Guarantee Scheme of Maharashtra, Unpublished dissertation, Indian Institute of Management, Bangalore, February.

FAO, 1987. *Report of the Inter-Agency Mission on Agrarian Reform and Rural Development*.

Lopez-Gonzaga, Violeta, 1988. *Government and Private Interventions among the Rural Workers of Negros: the Case of the Sugarcane Workers*, Research report for ILO-ARTEP, August.

Government of India, Ministry of Labour/National Commission on Rural Labour, 1990. *National Seminar on Agricultural Labour: Proceedings and Conclusions*.

Hart, Gillian, 1984. 'Agrarian labour arrangements and structural change: lessons from Java and Bangladesh', WEP Working Paper No. WEP-10-6/WP65, March.

Hirashima, S. and M. Muqtada, 1986. *Hired Labour and Rural Labour Markets in Asia*, ILO-ARTEP, New Delhi.

Hirway, Indira and J. Abraham, 1990. *Organising Rural Workers; The Gujarat Government Experience*, Oxford and IBH Publishing Co. Pvt. Ltd., New Delhi.

Hussain, Akmal, 1988. *Strategic Issues in Economic Policy*, Progressive Publishers, Lahore.

Hussain, Akmal, 1990. *Labour Absorption in Pakistan Agriculture* (mimeo.), study prepared for the GOP/ILO project on Employment and Manpower Strategies and Policies in Pakistan, ILO-ARTEP, New Delhi.

ILO, 1975. *Minimum wage fixing and economic development*, 3rd impression, Geneva.

ILO, 1985. *World Employment Programme Research in the 1980s*, Geneva.

ILO, 1988a. *Assessing the impact of statutory minimum wages in developing countries: four country studies*, Geneva.

ILO, 1988b. *Rural Employment Promotion*, Report VII, International Labour Conference, 75th Session, Geneva.

ILO, 1990. *Structure and functions of rural workers' organisations. A workers' education manual*, 2nd (revised) edition, Geneva.

ILO/ARPLA, 1987. *Labour inspection in agriculture in South Asia*, Asian and Pacific Regional Centre for Labour Administration, Bangkok.

ILO-ARTEP, 1987. *Structural Adjustment: By Whom, For Whom*, New Delhi.

Irfan, M., 1990. *Rural Employment and Wages in Pakistan*, Working Papers, ILO-ARTEP, New Delhi, May.

Jose, A.V., 1988. *Agricultural Wages in India*, ILO-ARTEP Working Paper, New Delhi.

Joshi, P.C., 1989. 'The Problem of Rural Labour in India Today: Some Reflections', *IASSI Quarterly*, Vol. 8 (2), September.

Kannan, K.P., 1990. *State and Union Intervention in Rural Labour: A Study of Kerala, India*, ARTEP Working Papers, ILO-ARTEP, New Delhi, July.

Department of Rural Development, India, 1988. National Seminar on Poverty Alleviation Programmes.

Mahmood, Moazam, 1991. *The implication of rural labour market analysis for generating rural employment in South Asia*, Working Papers, The Asian HRD Planning Network, ILO-ARTEP, New Delhi.

Mangahas, 1987. *Rural Employment Creation in the Philippines and Thailand*, in *ADB/ILO 1987*, 135–192.

Mazumdar, Dipak, 1989. 'Microeconomic Issues of Labor, Markets in Developing Countries: Analysis and Policy Implications', EDI Seminar paper No. 40, Economic Development Institute, The World Bank, Washington.

Mencher, Joan P., 1988. 'Peasants and agricultural labourers: an analytical assessment of issues involved in their organising', in T.N. Srinivasan and P.K. Bardhan (eds), *Rural Poverty in South Asia*, OUP, Delhi.

Ministry of Labour, Govt. of India, 1987. *Studying and reporting on the problems of unorganised workers in agriculture sector*, Report of the Sub-committee of the Parliamentary Consultative Committee.

Mukhopadhyay, Swapna, 1987. 'Intra-rural Labour Circulation in India: An Analysis', ARTEP Working Paper, ILO-ARTEP, New Delhi.

Muqtada, M. (ed), 1989. *The Elusive Target: An Evaluation of Target Group Approaches to Employment Creation in Rural Asia*, ILO-ARTEP, New Delhi.

NIRD, 1989. National Seminar on problems of rural labour and implementation of minimum wage laws: Reading Material (mimeo.), National Institute of Rural Development, Hyderabad.

Ofreneo, Rene E., 1990. 'Trade Unionism and Agrarian Reform in the Philippines, *Philippine Journal of Labour and Industrial Relations*, Vol. XII (2), 48–59.

Ofreneo, Rene E. and Melisa R. Serrano (eds), 1990. *Philippine Journal of Labour and Industrial Relations*, special issue on Trade Unionism and Agrarian Reform, Vol. xii (2).

Radwan, Samir, 1989. 'Preface to Special Issue on Rural Labour Markets and Poverty in Developing Countries', *International Labour Review*, Vol. 128(6), 681-84.

Ray, Shovan, 1987. 'Returns to Rural Labour in Asia', Working Paper, Rural Employment Policy Research Programme, ILO, Geneva.

Singh, Inderjit, 1990. *The great ascent: The rural poor in South Asia,* A World Bank Publication, The Johns Hopkins University Press, Baltimore, USA.

Singh, Karnail, 1987. Country Paper on India, in ILO/ARPLA, Labour Inspection in Agriculture in South Asia, Bangkok.

Stewart, Frances, 1987. 'Alternative Macro Policies, Meso Policies and Vulnerable groups' in UNICEF, *Structural Adjustment with a Human Face*, Vol. 1, 147-64.

Vyas, V.S., 1990. 'A Note on Employment Generation for Rural Labour: Approach and Strategies', in Government of India, Ministry of Labour, National Seminar on Agricultural Labour: Proceedings and Conclusions.

Wickramasekara, Piyasiri, 1987. 'Labour Absorption in Asian Agriculture: A Review of Findings', ILO-ARTEP Working Paper.

Wickramasekara, Piyasiri, 1990. 'Rural Employment Generation Schemes: Review of Asian Experiences', *Indian Journal of Industrial Relations*, Vol. 25 (4), April, 354–71.

Discussion

The principal discussant, Mr Jose Escartin from the Government of Philippines, broadly agreed with the theme that imperfections and distortions in rural labour markets can be remedied through conscious interventions. He cited the case of public works and other intervention programmes in the Phillippines which contributed to enhancing employment opportunities in the country. He also pointed out that minimum wage legislation for rural workers would eventually bring about an increase in wages and improvements in the social status of workers. However, wage fixation in such instances should strive to be more realistic taking into account productivity-related factors in the country-side. Also, the nature of inter-sectoral linkages in rural areas should be examined in the context of interventions for wage fixation. The discussant suggested that greater efforts should be made to study the rural labour markets in relation to their potential for employment generation by adequately taking into account the productivity and equity considerations.

The delegate from India commented on the paper with special reference to the rural wage employment programmes being undertaken in India and provided some updated information. He pointed that under the Jawahar Rozgar Yojana 1.6 million jobs are annually created in the country. These programmes have contributed towards bringing about a decline in under-employment and the rising wage rates of rural workers. In the absence of effective redistribution or land reforms, employment creation programmes of the above kind are the only instruments accessible to policy-makers for realising any substantial alleviation of poverty. Undoubtedly land improvements, afforestation schemes and special public works programmes which have been organised under the aegis of the state have had some visible effects in the Indian context. He, however, pointed out that in relative terms, the net impact of such employment creation programmes has been minimal. The Indian delegate also raised a query as to whether it is worthwhile spending large public funds on programmes for tackling under-employment in the country-side in a situation where unemployment is emerging as an even more crucial and important problem. In the long run, the country may have to divert resources towards promoting non-farm employment opportunities, which would be a more realistic approach for tackling the employment problem in the countryside.

The delegate from Bangladesh pointed out that interventions for fixing minimum wages should be linked to productivity levels prevailing in rural areas. The primary thrust of interventions should be to strengthen the asset position of rural workers He cited the success story of Grameen Bank in Bangladesh, which concentrated on a advancing credit to rural households at affordable rates of interest. The recovery rate of such credit advance has also been quite high in Bangladesh.

The Chinese delegate pointed out that interventions in rural areas have assumed special significance in China. The collapse of the commune system has necessitated the provision of special incentives to farmers along with transportation and housing arrangements in order to restrict the flow of migrant workers from rural areas. He argued that solutions have to be sought by minimising the income disparities prevalent in the country-side.

A representative of the employers' organisations from Thailand, while welcoming the case for interventions, pointed out that in the context of Thailand, the minimum wages are specified by a tripartite committee. He also mentioned that such wages tend to be too high and do not often reflect the capability of the employers to pay the prescribed wages.

The representative from Sri Lanka drew attention to an experiment being attempted in his country to facilitate the provision of working capital on credit to workers belonging to export-oriented production villages. The scheme caters to several grades of employees and makes arrangements to support the production teams by providing common facilities. Entrepreneurship training is also being provided by the government with a view to enhancing employment opportunities.

A representative of the Indian Labour Ministry commented on the structure of minimum wages prevailing in India. In Kerala state minimum wages are fixed through a tripartite body. He also pointed out that among Indian states, wages are found to be relatively higher in Kerala, so much so, that industries and employment are beginning to drift towards the neighbouring states. This has led to the demand for fixing minimum wages on a regional basis, rather than on the basis of individual states. In any case, there are problems in implementing prescribed minimum wages in many Indian states. In the matter of fixing minimum wages also, guidelines are often provided by the Central Government. Also, there are times when the courts in the country actively intervene in the fixation of minimum wages. The employers' representative from Pakistan also recommended adoption of a regional approach in fixing minimum wages.

Responding to the comments, Dr Wickramasekara pointed out that the purpose of the paper is not to make a case for across the board interventions in rural labour markets. Interventions ought to be contextual taking into account the socio-cultural factors in each country. Further, there is a case for promotion of rural non-farm employment opportunities in the long run. He agreed with the comments raised from the floor that the financial viability of large-scale investments for rural employment creation should be given due importance. An appropriate assessment of the costs and benefits of such investments should precede the design of such programmes. Dr Wickramasekara also emphasised that the tripartite forum should be promoted for fixation of minimum wages in rural areas.

5

ARTEP Work Programme for the Biennium 1992–93

Dr Rizwanul Islam, Director of ARTEP, started his presentation of the Programme of Work, 1992-93 by explaining that the ARTEP mandate relates to the ILO's World Employment Programme, of which ARTEP is a part. The objectives of the programme are to reduce unemployment, underemployment and poverty by creating productive employment and improving the distribution of income. Action-oriented research, advisory services and training are the means being adopted by the ARTEP in fulfilment of its mandate. Dr Islam noted that economic reform and structural adjustment are going on in many countries in the region, which adds an extra dimension to ARTEP's work. The Human Resource Development Approach is one way of easing the transition that these countries are undergoing. He then outlined three broad themes of work of which ARTEP will be focussing in the coming biennium, namely:

(a) Employment generation and poverty alleviation
(b) Economic reforms and structural adjustment
(c) Human resource development planning.

These themes may seem very broad, and the question is often asked whether ARTEP is spreading its resources too thinly. Then one has to consider the diversity and complexity of the countries in the Asian region, which makes it necessary for ARTEP to cover a broad range even as there is a need for prioritisation. Consequently, all items in the Work Programme cannot receive, and, indeed, do not require, equal attention, as in the fields in which ARTEP has already developed a certain competence.

It was also emphasised that the Programme of Work is not a list of projects, but an indication of themes that ARTEP would like to work with. They may, however, materialise into projects, subject to donor-funding. He added that the fifth UNDP inter-country programme will start next year and that ARTEP has already submitted project proposals for consideration. Dr Islam proceeded to spell out the work programme of the ARTEP. The main areas of work which will form the core of ARTEP's activities for the next two years are broadly:

1. Employment Planning and Labour Market Monitoring
2. Integrated Strategies for Employment Creation and Poverty Alleviation
3. Sectoral Employment Issues
4. Labour Markets and Human Resource Development
5. International Migration for Employment

The participants were then invited to provide their comments on the Programme of Work.

Discussion

The representative from India pointed out that ARTEP's work needs to be categorised according to the levels of development that exist among Asian countries. The second intervention from Malayasia pointed to the need for sub-regionalisation of programmes on the basis of labour shortage/labour surplus/unemployment, etc. In countries with a labour shortage problem, retraining and skills upgrading were of utmost importance to ensure job flexibility. He also suggested the inclusion of employment in the services sector in ARTEP's Programme of Work, as this is an important sector in fast-growing economies.

A Chinese participant agreed that the programme spreads over rather a wide area, and that priorities will have to be drawn up. He also requested for assistance in devising policies for rural non-farm activities, controlling rural-urban migration, implementing minimum wage policy and the wage index approach. Another important issue in China is female employment.

The participant from the Philippines suggested a country-level focus for ARTEP's programme and requested technical assistance for integrating greater employment planning in the Philippines development plan. The workers' representative from India requested ARTEP assistance in training programmes on HRD and technology upgrading for trade unions. Suggestions for assistance to the rural sector would be useful. The Indonesian government representative also pointed to the need for ARTEP to concentrate on a few key areas in view of its limited resources. Indonesia has a problem regarding the monitoring and evaluation of labour market information. The five year plans need to take into account training for data processing and dissemination of labour market information. ARTEP assistance towards training would be welcome.

The participant from the Ministry of Planning, Government of Pakistan, while quoting the *World Development Report* figures of 800 million people in poverty, suggested that poverty alleviation should receive the highest priority in ARTEP's work in view of the dimensions of the problem. New approaches and strategies were called for in this direction. A delegate from Thailand emphasised the need to create employment opportunities in the informal sector and for an income policy as wage differentials existed within the same employment group. He also requested assistance in the monitoring of labour market information and studies on wage fixation.

The participant from Mongolia pointed out that his country, being a centrally planned economy that was shifting its emphasis from macro- to micro-level planning, would benefit from the active cooperation of ARTEP in developing an information system and in the area of retraining. The employers' representative from Thailand pointed to the fact that ILO's budget for employers' association activities was less than 10 per cent and this figure could apply to ARTEP's policy as well. Hence, a strong case for assistance for employers' organisations was present. This point was endorsed by the employers' representative from Pakistan who also emphasised the need for ARTEP to find ways to include both employers and workers in the planning and implementation of their programmes. Since the informal sector offered the greatest opportunities for employment, ARTEP's studies would do well to concentrate on this sector.

A Sri Lankan participant suggested the inclusion in the Programme of Work of a section on impact of work done in the previous biennium and progress of projects, so that lessons can be learnt from failures as well as successes. The Nepal participant suggested assistance to build up non-governmental research organisations, and agreed on the importance of studying structural adjustment. He hoped ARTEP would take care not to duplicate work being done on migration.

A participant from Bangladesh commented on the need for developing and adopting appropriate technologies for employment promotion as the problem of labour shortage was not relevant to Bangladesh. A Laotian participant requested assistance in implementing reforms and understanding their effects on public-sector employment. The Bhutan delegate wholly supported ARTEP's Programme of Work.

In reply to the comments on ARTEP's capability and resources vis-a-vis the Programme of Work, Dr Islam said that a conscious effort would be made not to spread the limited resources too thinly. He noted that, priority had been given to structural adjustment, social dimensions, reforms in centrally planned economies, HRD planning, work on and for employers' organisations and trade unions and the informal sector. Dr Islam also agreed to include employment in the services sector and links between working conditions, productivity and employment in ARTEP's Work Programme. ARTEP would also be examining ways to operationalise an integrated approach to human resource development planning. Assistance to trade union researchers and dissemination of information on improved technologies would form important areas of ARTEP's activities. Exchange and dissemination of information on successful and innovative cases of micro-interventions for poverty alleviation would be given prominence in the Work Programme. Technical assistance to the erstwhile socialist economies would also taken up by ARTEP.

ANNEX

Fourth Meeting of Asian Employment Planners
New Delhi, Dec. 17-19, 1991

LIST OF PARTICIPANTS

Mr. Fasiul Alam Khan
Joint Secretary
Ministry of Labour and Manpower
Government of Bangladesh
Bangladesh Secretariat
Abdul Ghani Road
Dhaka
Bangladesh

Mr. Mohammad Mamdel Hossain
Deputy Chief
Planning Commission
Block 14, Room 18
General Economics Division
Macro & Perspective Planning Wing
Sher-E-Banglanagar
Dhaka
Bangladesh

Dasho Khandu Wangchuk
Secretary
Royal Civil Service Commission
Post Box No. 163
Taschichhodzong
Thimphu
Bhutan

Mr. HJ Zainal HJ Momin
Commissioner of Labour
Labour Department
4th Floor, Plaza Athirah
Jalan Kubah
Bandar Seri Begawan
Negara Brunei Darussalam
Brunei

Mr. Wang Dongyan
Deputy Director
Department of Overall Planning
Ministry of Labour
12 Hepingli Zhongjie
Beijing 100716
P.R. China

Mr. Wang Di
Division Chief
Social Development Department
State Planning Commission
38, South Street
Beijing
P.R. China, 100824

Mr. Narendra Singh
Research Consultant
Indian National Metalworkers Federation
    (INTUC)
26-K Road
Jamshedpur - 831 001
India

Dr. Trilok Singh Papola
Adviser
Labour, Employment and Manpower
205, Yojana Bhavan
Planning Commission
Parliament Street
New Delhi - 110 001
India

Mr. Jagdish Joshi
Director-General of Employment &
   Training
Directorate General of Employment &
   Training
Ministry of Labour
Government of India
Shram Shakti Bhavan
Rafi Marg
New Delhi - 110 001
India

Mr. Moedjiman
Head, Bureau of Planning
Ministry of Manpower
Jl. Jend. gatot Subroto Kav:51
Jakarta
Indonesia

Mr. Lucky Firnandy Majanto
Staff Bureau of Manpower
National Development Planning Agency
   (BAPPENAS)
Jl. Taman Suropati No.2
Jakarta 10310
Indonesia

Mr. Sisouvanh Tandavong
Deputy Director
Labour Department
Ministry of Economics, Planning and
   Finance
Vientiane
LAOS PDR

Mr. Yau De Piyau
Director of Research and Planning
Ministry of Human Resources
Level 3, Block B North
Jalan Damanlela
Pusat Bandar Damansara
50530 Kuala Lumpur
Malaysia

Mr. Rabbi P Royan
Principal Assistant Director
Economic Planning Unit
Prime Minister's Department
Jalan Dato Onn
50502 Kuala Lumpur
Malaysia

Mr. Ishen Batbavar
Ministry of Foreign Relations
Ulaan Batar
Mongolia

Dr. Rabindra Kumar Shakya
Additional Secretary
National Planning Commission
Singha Durbar
Kathmandu
Nepal

Mr. Dev Ratna Tamrakar
Deputy Director
Ministry of Labour & Social Welfare
Department of Labour
Ramshah Path
Putalisadak
Kathmandu
Nepal

Mr. Safdar Hussain Kazmi
Secretary
Ministry of Labour, Manpower and
   Overseas Pakistanis
Pakistan Secretariat
Block 'B'
Islamabad
Pakistan

Dr. Akhtar Hasan Khan
Secretary
Ministry of Planning and Development
Planning and Development Division
Block 'P' Room No. 202
Pakistan Secretariat
Islamabad
Pakistan

Mr. Ahsan Ullah Khan
Director
Shahsons (Private) Limited
D/88, S.I.T.E., Manghopir Road
Karachi - 75700
Pakistan

Ms. Cesarina B. Rejante
Assistant Director General
National Economic & Development
    Authority
5th Floor NEDA Bldg.
Amber Avenue, Pasig
Metro Manila
Philippines

Mr. Jose Escartin
Deputy Director General
National Manpower & Youth Council
Fort Bonifacio, Taguig
Metro Manila
Philippines

Mr. H.M. Gunasekera
Deputy Director
Department of National Planning
Ministry of Policy Planning &
    Implementation
General Treasury Building
Colombo 1
Sri Lanka

Mr. Bertie Liyanamana
Secretary to State Minister for Labour
Ministry of Labour and Vocational
    Training
Labour Secretariat
Narahondita
Colombo 5
Sri Lanka

Mr. Bhichai Reenbheyawon
Executive Director
Employers' Confederation of Thailand
937-939 Sukhumvit 51
Prakranong
Bangkok
Thailand

Mrs. Vacharee Sinthuvanich
Chief
Employment and Wage Sector
Human Resources Planning Division
National Economic and Social
    Development Board
962 Krung Kasem Road
Bangkok 10120
Thailand

Ms. Mallika Kunnavatana
Director
Labour Statistics and Planning Division
Labour Department
Fuangnakorn Road
Bangkok 10200
Thailand

Dr. Martin Godfrey
Institute of Development Studies
Brighton
U.K.

ILO, Geneva
Dr. Rashid Amjad

ILO-ROAP, Bangkok
Mr. J.M. Servais

ILO-ARTEP, New Delhi
Dr. Rizwanul Islam
Dr. A.V. Jose
Dr. M. Muqtada
Dr. A.K. Ghose
Dr. Piyasiri Wickramasekara
Mr. Peter Duiker (ARTEP Focal Point,
    Bangkok)
Ms. A. Hildeman
Ms. Usha Tankha
Mr. A.K. Vasisht
Ms. Sophy Jacob
Mr. P. Gopi Krishna